China's One Belt One Road

Initiative, Challenges and Prospects

China's One Belt One Road

Initiative, Challenges and Prospects

Edited By

Bal Krishan Sharma & Nivedita Das Kundu

(Established 1870)

United Service Institution of India
New Delhi

in collaboration with

Sichuan University
Chengdu

Vij Books India Pvt Ltd

New Delhi (India)

Published by

Vij Books India Pvt Ltd
(Publishers, Distributors & Importers)
2/19, Ansari Road
Delhi – 110 002
Phones: 91-11-43596460, 91-11-47340674
Fax: 91-11-47340674
e-mail: vijbooks@rediffmail.com

Copyright © 2016, United Service Institution of India, New Delhi

| ISBN | : 978-93-85563-59-1 (Hardback) |
| ISBN | : 978-93-85563-60-7 (ebook) |

Contents

Appendices

List of Figures

Preface

This Book is the outcome of a Joint research conducted by the scholars from United Service Institution of India (USI), Center for Strategic Studies and Simulation (CS3) and Sichuan University (SCU), Faculty of Social Development and Western China Development Studies,(FSDWCDS) on the topic "China's One Belt One Road: Initiative, Challenges and Prospects". In the recent years, the Chinese side has accorded a very high priority to 'One Belt One Road', (OBOR) in its economic and foreign policy matrices. The aim of this joint-research publication is to bring out both Indian and Chinese perspectives in one collection. Therefore, the chapters in this book narrate various viewpoints, opportunities, concerns and challenges of the OBOR and provide both Indian and Chinese perspective of the subject. A key idea that has emerged from this volume is that national development goals and interest of India and China should be addressed in a mutually supportive manner. Further, there is a need to show respect, sensitivity, interest for each other's aspirations. The chapters also emphasized the concern that unilateral decisions may not auger well in the connectivity projects as it interlinks nations. Hence, collaborative and consultative approaches tend to work better. This is more so, in Asia with the absence of agreed security architecture. This makes transparency in such a project desirable with constructive deliberations on choice of specific routes, on the alignment, approaches, providing rationale behind choices. Being transnational initiative with a large scope, issues related to the international norms and on legal concerns needs to be jointly examined and mutually agreed to.

The research queries addressed in the Chapters of these volume articulate contours of OBOR as proposed by the Chinese side and examine India's point of view on OBOR. This Book is therefore divided into two sections. The first section describes the "One Belt One Road: China's Perspective" by the academics from SCU and the second section deals with "One Belt One Road: India's Perspective", by the scholars from USI.

It is expected that this Book will fill in existing gap in the literature on this subject and provide useful inputs to policy planners. The readers will find important information on both Chinese and Indian perspectives and respective positions on issues and concerns related to China's OBOR initiative.

It is important to note that the discussions on connectivity should address not only the physical infrastructure aspects but also the institutional, digital, financial, as well as commercial aspects in detail as there is a need to provide clarity on how the Institutions are going to coalesce in initial building and subsequent management of this ambitious connectivity and transportation project. These demand statecraft and sagacity of a unique order to reconcile different point of views.

China understandably has mooted Indian participation in OBOR initiative. A dispassionate study of this proposal highlights its potential to integrate the Asian economic landscape. However, the contour of OBOR in regard to politico-economic and security aspects merit a greater examination and debate. Prima facie there are areas of convergence and divergence in Indian and Chinese perspectives on the subject, which need to be explained in the light of contemporary and vexed bilateral relations.

On behalf of USI, I express my sincere gratitude to the scholars and academics from USI and SCU for enthusiastically collaborating in this joint publication and for providing their valuable inputs and penning down their precious thoughts and understanding on the topic of OBOR.

Lt. Gen. P.K. Singh (Retd.)
Director United Service Institution of India, New Delhi

Acknowledgement

This Book is part of a joint project between United Service Institution of India (USI) and Sichuan University, (SCU) Chengdu, China, under the Memorandum of Understanding (MOU) agreement signed by both the Institutes. While working on this joint project the authors from both India and China supported each other for collecting research material, providing information and inputs through discussions and conferences.

We sincerely thank Director USI, Lt Gen PK Singh for his unwavering support and encouragement. We also take this opportunity to thank USI colleagues who was always there with their supportive and cooperative attitude for successfully conducting this project.

We also take this opportunity to thank Prof. Yang Minghong and Dr. Huang Yunsong from SCU for conducting sincere research on the topic and for their cooperative approach. They shared some insightful and thought-provoking ideas in their Chapters.

Last but not the least; we would like to take this opportunity to thank USI's administrative and academic staff of the Center for Strategic Studies and Simulation's (CS3) for their encouragement and support. It is entirely due to the whole-hearted cooperation and assistance by both the Indian and Chinese side this volume has taken the present shape.

New Delhi   **Bal Krishna Sharma & Nivedita Das Kundu**

Contributors

Nivedita Das Kundu, PhD, in International Studies, is Senior Research Advisor with United Service Institution of India, New Delhi. Her research expertise focuses on geopolitics, geo-economics, foreign policy, multilateral organisations, border issues, migration and strategic dimensions of security. Dr. Nivedita has worked extensively on Silk Route and transport corridor issues and concerns. She has contributed widely and worked on her research expertise with prestigious International Universities and research Institutes/Think Tanks in India and abroad. She has authored and edited books, Monographs and published research articles on her area of research.

Yang Minghong, PhD, in Economics, is Professor, Executive Director, Faculty of Social Development and Western China Development Studies, Sichuan University, Chengdu. Prof. Yang is a leading Chinese scholar on China Studies, Tibetan Studies, and South Asian Studies. His current work is covering Regional Economics, Borderlands Studies, Tibet Development, and exiled-Tibetan issue. He has contributed extensively in the international academic circle.

Huang Yunsong, PhD, International Law, is Associate Professor, Faculty of Social Development and Western China Development Studies, Sichuan University, Chengdu,. Dr. Huang's expertise is on strategic, politico- security issues and concerns related to South Asian studies and international law. Dr. Huang pioneered the understanding of some critical issues in China-India relations such as the exiled Tibetans in India and border dispute.

MH Rajesh, alumnus of Naval Academy and Defence Services Staff College. Cdr Rajesh is Research Fellow with United Service Institution of India, New Delhi. He is a Submariner and has specialized in Anti-Submarine Warfare. He has expertise on Maritime security & Strategic Studies. He is presently working on the research topic on Chinese Maritime Strategy in Indian Ocean Region and Implications for the India's Maritime Security Engagement in the Region.

Abbreviations

ACD	Asia Cooperation Dialogue
AIIB	Asian Infrastructure Investment Bank
ALTID	Asian Land Transport Infrastructure Development
APEC	Asia-Pacific Economic Cooperation
ASEAN	Association for the South-East Asian Nations
ASEM	Asia-Europe Meeting
BCIM	Bangladesh-China-India-Myanmar
BRICS	Brazil, Russia, India, China and South Africa
CAREC	Central Asia Regional Economic Cooperation
CASCF	China-Arab States Cooperation Forum
CICA	Conference on Interaction and Confidence-Building Measures in Asia
CPEC	China-Pakistan Economic Corridor
ERP	European Recovery Program
GMS	Greater Mekong Sub-region
IAGS	Analysis of Global Security
INSTC	International North-South Transport Corridor
IOR	Indian Ocean region
LAC	Line of Actual Control

MSR	Maritime Silk Road
NSRF	New Silk Road Fund
OBOR	One Belt One Road
OECD	Organisation for Economic Co-operation and Development
ReCAAP	Regional Cooperation Agreement on Combatting Piracy and Armed robbery against ships in Asia
SCO	Shanghai Cooperation Organization
SCU	Sichuan University
SREB	Silk Road Economic Belt
TAPI	Turkmenistan-Afghanistan-Pakistan-India
TASIM	Trans-Eurasian Information Super Highway
TPP	Trans-Pacific Partnership
UNCLOS	United Nations Convention on the Law of the Sea
UNSC	United Nations Security Council
WTO	World Trade Organisation

Introduction

Nivedita Das Kundu

'One Belt One Road', Unfolding Challenges and Opportunities for India-China Cooperation

German Geographer, Ferdinand von Richthofen in 1877 termed 'Seidenstrabe' or 'Silk Road', for the first time.

The great Silk Road not only developed and enhanced trade and commerce between the East and the West, but also developed significant factor in facilitating cultural and social interaction across continents. The "One Belt One Road" (OBOR) initiative announced by China's President Xi Jinping is a proposal to revive the ancient Silk Road. The OBOR is an ambitious connectivity project; under the OBOR initiative China introduced an economic model that seeks to shift the site and purpose of development even outside China. Under the OBOR initiative China proposes the construction of a series of transportation platforms along the ancient Silk Road that will connect China with Central Asia, Europe and West Asia. This outward thrust of investment and capital construction envisages significant reduction of distance between China and the world that will form a road traversing different geographies of nations, territories and cultures connecting East with the West.

The basic principle of OBOR is to enhance connectivity through multi-model transport corridors weather on 'land' or through 'Sea' that lead to economic integration, free flow of goods and services that enhances trade, commerce, economic activity including promotion of people to people exchanges. The OBOR has continental and maritime components. The maritime route connects important ports in China, the South China Sea, and the Indian Ocean, with the European ports in the Mediterranean Sea. The continental route links-up western China with Central Asia and

Europe. However, it is also an imperative that wherever there is an economic interaction there is bound to be a degree of geo-politics too. Even in the era of globalisation though the dominant theme is geo-economics the geo-political, geo-strategic aspects of the evolving economic world order also comes into play.

The thinking behind the 'Belt' and 'Road' strategy as defined by Chinese government is an 'initiative' and not as a 'plan' or 'strategy'. By putting forward various proposals through OBOR initiative, China is hoping to find partners willing to cooperate and participate in the China's OBOR initiative. OBOR initiative can also be considered as a transnational connectivity model, as it aims to coordinate factors of economic circulation across different national spaces, with different governance models, legal norms and political contingencies. Centuries ago the original trading route was contiguous territory where boundaries remained too fluid for any authorities to impose its will, but today, the OBOR route is an imagined geography as this route is controlled by sovereign national territorial states having effective authority structures over each of these units. Hence, today the OBOR initiative requires China to entail a broad-based economic coordination with diverse governance system moreover, transparency needs to be maintained.

The debate on the OBOR initiative by China focuses on and anticipates possible policy convergence between China and other Sovereign national governments along the road. The construct of the OBOR is a consequence of the rapid rise of China and it seeks to revive old trading routes and in some cases even create new trading routes across various countries. Currently, the OBOR plans to plug into South Asia in a significant manner. Similarly, the 'Maritime Silk Road' (MSR) initiative seeks to develop port connectivity. Under the OBOR initiative 'Maritime Silk Road Economic Belt' and 'Maritime Silk Road' highlighted its salient features for improving connectivity and infrastructure, trade and economic activity, enhanced cooperation in industrial investment, development of resources of energy, financial cooperation, people to people exchanges, environmental cooperation and cooperation in maritime affairs.

This Book is the outcome of the research essays written and compiled by United Service Institution of India's (USI) scholars along with the academics from the Faculty of Social Development and Western China

Development Studies, Sichuan University (SCU). The authors tried to highlight India's and China's viewpoint on "One Belt One Road", both on 'Land' and on 'Maritime' routes. The Emphasis of the research essays contributed by the Indian experts provides India's perspective on the "One Belt One Road". The essays written by experts from China covered various dimensions and shared views and concerns related to 'One Belt One Road' from China's perspective. However, all authors shared possible convergence and divergences of ideas too. Simultaneously, a critical assessment was also highlighted and weak points were also discussed and identified by the authors in the essays. The authors also discussed on the prospective spheres of cooperation through OBOR initiative. The academic analyses given by the experts combined recommendations with concrete measures suggested to overcome the obstacles and differences. The Chapters also highlighted the importance of connectivity and network overview from the regional perspectives. The Chapters also tried to examine and debate various aspects providing literary discourses and present dynamics of the region focussing on possible challenges.

This can also reduce barriers to develop mutual trust and confidence. The key idea is to bring forth the insights, which helps in understanding the new geo-political reality and improve possible regional cooperation. The research questions that authors attempted to address while working on their respective chapters are mainly to understand, What is "One Belt One Road' initiative?, Is it China's economic initiative or strategy?, what will be the OBOR's implications for South Asia?, What will be the role of other regional countries in OBOR initiative? How India can benefit from OBOR?, What are the security concerns of OBOR? What are the geostrategic implication and challenges? What is the economic significance of OBOR? What is the regional discourse on OBOR, focussing both on the Land and Sea routes? What are the major points of convergence between India and China on the OBOR? On the whole, in this volume the authors tried to put forward optimism giving positive approach. India and China's interest have always tended to coincide as far as trade and economic cooperation is concerned.[1] India is eager for high growth opportunity in the coming years and OBOR has got the potential to provide such option, however, on certain security concerns differences of approach on specific issues were also emphasized in this volume, however, the overall parallelism of interest has also been highlighted.

The authors highlighted that "One Belt One Road" initiative includes multifaceted cooperation aimed at constructing a community of shared destiny. Nonetheless, is a need to strengthen the trust factor for playing major role in the region by both the Nations as well as for making the regionalism a successful connotation? The Chapters in this volume touched upon various policy objectives providing insight into the reality. The theme of the chapters dexterously worked out with well documented data based on original sources, thus, this Book on "China's One Belt One Road: Initiative, Challenges and Prospects," has got the potential to provide a broad idea and clarity on this contemporary policy relevant topic under study.

Endnotes

1   In-spite of persistent differences on boundary dispute, China and India has robust economic interactions. In 2014, the India-China bilateral trade stood at $71.53 billion. Way back in 1984, India and China accorded each other 'Most Favoured Nation' (MFN) status.

Section I

One Belt One Road: China's Perspective

1

Understanding the One Belt One Road Initiative: China's Perspective

Yang Minghong

Over the past 2000 years, the Silk Road has been expanding on the world map, telling inspiring stories of people to people exchange and mutual benefits among the countries. Recently, the revival of the great Silk Road spirit has become a guiding post for the world political and economic fields with the peaceful rise of China. From China's perspective, there are several clarifications that need to be addressed. When discuss about the "Belt and Road Initiative", many think tanks and scholars relate it to the concept of "economic corridor". It is necessary to introduce and elaborate relevant facts in accordance with the official and authoritative document Vision and Actions on Jointly Building Silk Road Economic Belt and 21st-Century Maritime Silk Road (hereafter referred to as the Vision and Actions).

OBOR is an Initiative or strategy?

After the proposal of the 'Belt and Road' Initiative, many overseas media and think tanks refer to it as a "strategy". The use of the word "strategy" suggests that China wants to pursue the benefits of the Belt and Road Initiative exclusively from the perspective of its own national interests and it is even a game strategy targeting certain countries.

According to China's official and authoritative document the Vision and the Actions, the proposal of the Belt and Road Initiative is indeed a strategic vision, however, the deeper meaning of the vision is that China should face the changes, opportunities and challenges in the open economy, analyze the new directions and new routes of the economic globalization and re-evaluate China's new round of opening up policies with a coordinated perspective that focus on the world and domestically so as to promote China's foreign trade cooperation in different regions to develop within a broader scope, wider fields at a higher level.

As a strategic vision, the 'Belt and Road' Initiative is distinctly different both internally and externally.

Externally, there is only the saying of jointly building the 'Belt and Road' Initiative and no such saying as the Belt and Road Strategy, because this initiative emphasizes that the 'Belt and Road' Initiative is not an entity or mechanism but an idea and initiative that focuses on cooperation and development. It relies on the existing multi-lateral mechanism between China and relevant countries and borrows the existing and effective regional cooperation platforms with the aim of holding high the banner of peaceful development, proactively developing economic and cooperative partnership with countries along the road reviving the ancient silk road, cooperatively building the communities of common interests, common destiny and common responsibilities featuring political mutual trust, economic integration and cultural tolerance. From the common demands of the countries along the Belt and the Road, Chinese government holds that, the Belt and Road Initiative matches the needs of these countries to pursue fast development and can create new windows of opportunities for these countries to identify complementary advantages and pursue opening up and development.

Internally, the 'Belt and Road' Initiative is a new strategy that China adopts to further promote opening up. Over the past 30 years, China has made tremendous achievements in opening up, however, due to reasons of geographic location, resources endowment and development foundation, the opening up has presented a pattern featuring the fast development of the east and slower development of the west and strong development of the coastal areas and weak development of the inlands. The 'Belt' in the Belt and Road Initiative puts the inlands at the front of the development and the 'Road' becomes the forefront of the eastern opening up. In this way, an all-round opening up has been formed to promote China's reform and development through opening up. Countries along the 'Belt and Road' Initiative are mostly emerging economies and developing countries with a total population of 4.4 billion and an economic aggregate of 21 trillion

US dollars, accounting for 63% and 29% of the world's total respectively. These countries are usually in the upward phase of economic development and enjoy broad prospects of mutually beneficial cooperation. By digging the cooperation potential between China and these countries, emerging economies and developing countries will enjoy higher status in China's opening-up pattern. It will also promote the opening up of China's central and western regions and the border areas boost eastern coastal areas to upgrade their open economy so as to formulate a new open and global pattern featuring the coordination of the coast and the inlands, and the eastern and the western regions. Chinese government holds that realizing bilateral opening up and cooperation with the countries along the Belt and Road is not only beneficial for these countries but also conducive to China. As a result, it is a progressive and open strategy.

From the latter aspect, as an opening up strategy, the Belt and Road Initiative prompted some illusions of domestic think tanks; they confuse the external initiative and the internal strategy and misunderstand it as an external strategy. Through the construction of the 'Belt and Road' Initiative, the political and economic cooperation between China and other Asian and European countries will be strengthened and meanwhile, the competition with other major countries will probably emerge and may become fiercer. For instance, most of the central Asian countries are EU's trading partners, investment and energy suppliers and Russia's long-term backyard. Although China does not hope to seek dominance in regional affairs and does not create sphere of influence, the contention between China, EU and the US is unavoidable. This situation might appear with south Asian countries, but it is an objective circumstance that might occur and it is different from the subjective vision that China proposes.

It is worth mentioning that many domestic think tanks and academic research institutes also use the term 'Belt and Road Strategy'. It is true However, among all the official documents concerning foreign relations we found, the word "strategy" has never been used. The most frequent use is "strategic vision". It is the provinces in China that connect "strategy" with "Belt and Road Initiative". In fact, since China implements reform and opening up, the word "strategy" has been used to refer to using a systematic planning to perform a certain kind of work, instead of adopting hostile measures targeting relevant sides.

What is the Chinese Version of the Marshall Plan?

Many media and think tanks from home and abroad connect the Belt and Road Initiative with the European Recovery Program, ERP (also known as the Marshall Plan) and name it the Chinese Marshall Plan, suggesting that the Belt and Road Initiative is an aggressive strategy.

The Origin of Reintroducing the Marshall Plan

Since the Global Financial Crisis in 2008, serious surplus capacity appeared in China. The internationalization of RMB has also become an urgent matter.

As early as February 2009, then vice president and the chief economist of the World Bank (now professor of Peking University), Justin Lin also proposed a "world recovery plan with the Marshall Plan spirit". He suggested that the developed countries and countries with huge foreign reserves invest 2 trillion US dollars in the next 5 years in the bottle neck projects of the developing countries such as the infrastructure so as to promote world economic recovery. On October 19th 2012, Justin Lin further explained that the "New Marshall Plan" gave room for developed countries to conduct structural reform, i.e. increase the export demand of the developed countries by investing in the world infrastructure; this investment is a win-win project, developed countries can ride over financial crisis though structural reform and developing countries can remove their infrastructure bottleneck and gain opportunities for faster development.[1]

In November 2014, during the APEC (Beijing) Summit, when the news of China establishing "Asian Infrastructure Investment Bank" and "Silk Road Fund" was released, many research institutes and media use "China's Marshall Plan" to describe the so called China's "major strategy": Asian Infrastructure Investment Bank is an important guarantee of China's Marshall Plan; the 'Belt and Road' Initiative is a strategic vehicle for China's capital export plan. Capital export can digest its excess capacity, boost the infrastructure construction of emerging economies and the least developed countries and promote global growth. The article "The Belt and Road Initiative accelerates Asia-Pacific connectivity, China's Marshall Plan Launches" by Huaxia Daily made the name "China's Marshall Plan" prevalent. [2]

The differences between the Marshall Plan and the Belt and Road Initiative

Firstly, the background and the aims are different; the Marshall Plan was closely connected with the Cold War. The Second World War caused huge disasters to Europe. It was not only casualty, but also the collapse of infrastructure. The drained national treasuries of the countries involved and the severe natural disasters determined that Europe cannot go out of the shadow of the war without external aid. With the purpose of helping Europe to recover, digesting domestic capacity and curbing the Soviet Union and Eastern Europe Group, the US implemented the so called Marshall Plan. The background and aims of the 'Belt and Road' Initiative are made very clear in the Vision and the Actions. The background is embracing the trend towards a multipolar world, economic globalization, cultural diversity and greater IT application and the aim is promoting orderly and free flow of economic factors, highly efficient allocation of resources and deep integration of markets; encouraging the countries along the Belt and Road to achieve economic policy coordination and carry out broader and more in-depth regional cooperation of higher standards; and jointly creating an open, inclusive and balanced regional economic cooperation architecture that benefits all. The US has already established its dominant economic status when implementing the Marshall Plan. In comparison, the per capita GDP of China is still below 8000 US dollars, well below the world average, so China does not have the advantages that the US enjoyed at the beginning of the Second World War. This determined that the Belt and Road Initiative cannot be a large scale international aid plan and will not form a new round of "Cold War".

Secondly, Different strategic connotations the Marshall Plan, the US provided economic aid to OECD countries in various forms. More subtly, the US intentionally penetrates its political ideology to the European countries through economic aid and pushed the development of the Cold War. The 'Belt and Road' Initiative that China advocates uses capital export to enter the Asia-Pacific and the Europe and establishes an all-round opening pattern across the Eurasia. It will not promote the development of the Cold War pattern. China reiterates the importance of a multilateral trading system and emphasizes that its participation and launch of the regional economic integration are compatible and complementary to the multilateral trading system. The countries and regions covered by the

'Belt and Road' Initiative go beyond the Asia-Pacific FTA. As the Vision and Actions states, The 'Belt and Road' Initiative aims to promote the connectivity of Asian, European and African continents and their adjacent seas, establish and strengthen partnerships among the countries along the Belt and Road, set up all-dimensional, multi-tiered and composite connectivity networks, and realize diversified, independent, balanced and sustainable development in these countries. The Marshall Plan focused on the economic recovery of countries who had advanced foundation and sound system after the damage of productivity, while the Belt and Road Initiative emphasizes the building of countries who are at a low level of development, and even countries with defective systems and mechanisms as well as defective legal guarantees in the following five areas: policy coordination, facilities connectivity, unimpeded trade, financial integration and people-to-people bonds. The aim is to promote orderly and free flow of economic factors, highly efficient allocation of resources and deep integration of markets.

Thirdly, Different cooperation models, the Marshall Plan targeted the economic recovery of European countries and did not involve developing countries, while the countries along the 'Belt and Road' are mostly emerging economies and developing countries. In the Marshall Plan, the US lent two thirds of the gold reserve to the recipient countries and requested them to purchase certain products from the US so that the US can transfer the excess capacity into creditor's rights, in this way, the US not only avoided economic recession after the World War II, but also opened the global golden age of growth. The 'Belt and Road' Initiative first started with large scale infrastructure construction, the development and utilization of resources and energy and all round trade service exchange, which will bring more industry chains and investment opportunities for the capital market. The Vision and the Actions states that China's economy is closely connected with the world economy. China will stay committed to the basic policy of opening-up, build a new pattern of all-round opening-up, and integrate itself deeper into the world economic system," and "China is committed to shouldering more responsibilities and obligations within its capabilities, making greater contributions to the peace and development of mankind.

Fourth, Different implementation mechanisms, the Marshall Plan that the US implemented had a very strong feature of administrative order, while the 'Belt and Road' Initiative stresses market cooperation. As stated in the Vision and the Actions, the Initiative follows market operation. It will abide by market rules and international norms, give play to the decisive role of the market in resource allocation and the primary role of enterprises, and let the governments perform their due functions. In the 'Belt and Road' Initiative, China does not use China's Ministry of Finance as the sole implementation agency but promoted the establishment of regional development agencies such as Asian Infrastructure Investment Bank (AIIB) and Silk Road Fund to serve as the main implementers. China also does not seek control within the AIIB and the Silk Road Fund like what the US did in the International Monetary Fund and the World Bank. An Indian serving as the president of the BRICS Development Bank indicates that China does not have the intention to control these international economic organizations; instead, China will work in accordance with the international rules. This attitude will be further proved in the launch and operation of the AIIB and the Silk Road Fund.

Different Voice of the International Community

Although some media and think tanks refer to the 'Belt and Road' Initiative as China's Marshall Plan, there are different voice in the international community.

For example, ShaZukang, the former UN under Secretary General and Secretary General for UN Division for Sustainable Development, thinks that the background idea and the practice of the Belt and Road Initiative are completely different from the Marshall Plan. China has stressed again and again that the 'Belt and Road' Initiative should be jointly built through consultation to meet the interests of all.[3]

Another view point expressed by Gal Luft, co-director of the Institute for the Analysis of Global Security (IAGS) and a senior adviser to the United States Energy Security Council, thinks that the 'Belt and Road' Initiative and the Marshall Plan are not comparable. The Marshall Plan was to reconstruct Europe after the war and it was a purely American plan. The 'Belt and Road' Initiative, however, is not only a Chinese plan. It is proposed by China who hopes and welcomes more participants. He also thinks that the 'Belt and Road' Initiative is not a temporary plan, but will involve one and more generations and can even go beyond the century, while the Marshall Plan only used several decades to help Europe to recover.

As a result, the 'Belt and Road' Initiative will operate at a different pace and will be disturbed by some factors, for example, the economic recession in some countries and also diseases might affect its growth, hence, there is a need to have patience.

Is through OBOR China transferring excess capacity?

Excess capacity is a big problem facing China, so many scholars and think tanks regard the Belt and Road Initiative as China's plan to transfer excess capacity. There is a thought that it is possible to transfer the excess capacity through the 'Belt and Road', Initiative, but there is a need to understand this issue dialectically.

Firstly, the fast development of economic globalization has already provided conditions for China to transfer excess capacity. There is no national boundary in enterprises' development. The nature to pursue profits enables them to regard the world as their investment destination. The economy is influenced by globalization and the rapid development of world economic integration, so even if China did not propose the Belt and Road Initiative, China's excess capacity will be transferred to other countries. This is an objective economic principle. It means that as long as the countries along the Belt and Road do not refuse economic globalization, they would not refuse China's transfer of excess capacity to them; China did not propose the Belt and Road Initiative to transfer the excess capacity.

Secondly, even if the Belt and Road Initiative provides an effective way for China to solve the excess capacity problem, and it also gives opportunities for the recipient countries to develop. The process of economic development is the combination of production factors. Countries and regions along the Belt and Road are still in the preliminary phase of economic development, so it is common to lack capital and technology. There is a huge need for necessary means of production and consumption of goods. China's transfer of capital, technology, means of production and means of livelihood to these countries and regions and can help them to boost local economic development. In fact, in the past 30 years, China realized huge economic development by receiving the capacity transferred from Europe, the US, and emerging economies and regions in Asia. The Flying Geese Paradigm concluded by Japanese Economist Kaname Akamatsu suggests that the countries along the Belt and Road can develop domestic market by importing, absorbing and digesting technologies and equipment.

Thirdly, the Belt and Road Initiative does not give extra economic guarantee to enterprises to transfer capacity. According to the vision of the Belt and Road Initiative, the plan should operate according to the market and internationally practiced rules. All of the projects should adopt international business rules. Whether Chinese enterprises will obtain the contracting rights of the projects and the purchasing rights of the equipment and materials in the bidding depends on their competitiveness. Even though some enterprises won the bidding and transferred the capacity overseas, it is a result of competition, not a result of special treatment or institutional arrangement. From the perspective of institutional arrangement, it is impossible for China to do such arrangement just for capacity transfer.

OBOR Transparency

Many Indian scholars think that the Belt and Road Initiative has very low transparency, so people could not see the conspiracy targeting certain countries and other countries cannot find the entrance to participate, however, this is a huge misunderstanding.

Chinese government has introduced and explained the Initiative once and once again to remove the misunderstanding. On September 7th, 2013, President Xi Jinping delivered a speech at Nazarbayev University in Kazakhstan and elaborated on "taking an innovative approach" and "starting work in individual areas and link them up over time to cover the whole region" and "jointly building an "economic belt along the Silk Road". On October 3rd, 2013, President Xi Jinping made a speech at the Indonesian Parliament and elaborated on the approach of "strengthening maritime cooperation with ASEAN countries, making full use of the China-ASEAN Maritime Cooperation Fund to develop maritime cooperation partnership" and jointly building 21st Century Maritime Silk Road. In March 2015, authorized by the State Council of China, the National Development and Reform Commission, Ministry of Foreign Affairs and Ministry of Commerce of the People's Republic of China jointly issued the Vision and the Actions. This is a guiding document for the 'Belt and Road' Initiative. On March 28th, 2015, State Councillor Yang Jiechi further explained the jointly built 21st Century Maritime Silk Road on the Boao Forum for Asia 2015, Annual Conference.

It can be inferred that the relevant policies in the Belt and Road Initiative are transparent. It is necessary to understand the transparency from the policy itself.

Firstly, from the overall framework of jointly building the Belt and Road Initiative, the main aim is to build two economic trade and transport routes. Chinese government proposes that on land, the Initiative will focus on jointly building a new Eurasian Land Bridge and developing China-Mongolia-Russia, China-Central Asia-West Asia and Indochina Peninsula economic corridors by taking advantage of international transport routes, relying on core cities along the Belt and Road and using key economic industrial parks as cooperation platforms. At sea, the Initiative will focus on jointly building smooth, secure and efficient transport routes connecting major sea ports along the Belt and Road. The AIIB, BRICS Development Bank and the Silk Road Fund provided strong material basis for the infrastructure construction of the countries along the Belt and the Road.

Secondly, from the cooperation scope, the priority fields for the Initiative are transportation connectivity, trade facilitation and people to people exchange. China proposed that countries along the 'Belt and Road' have their own resource advantages and their economies are mutually complementary. Therefore, there is a great potential and space for cooperation. They should promote policy coordination, facilitate connectivity, unimpeded trade, financial integration and people-to-people bonds as their five major goals. On March 28th, 2015, state councillor Yang Jiechi noted on the Boao Forum for Asia 2015 Annual Conference that "in addition to maritime transport and resource development, OBOR will involve research, environmental protection, tourism, disaster reduction and prevention, law enforcement cooperation and people-to-people exchanges on the sea. Not only will it look at the development of the blue economy and building of oceanic economic demonstration zones offshore, it will also build onshore industrial parks, marine science and technology parks and training bases for ocean-related personnel. OBOR initiative will not only utilizing the oceanic resources, this will also protect the oceanic environment. This will deliver a good life to the people along the coast; we should also bring about an interconnected development of the hinterland and coastal regions to achieve common prosperity.

Thirdly, from the ways of cooperation, countries along the Belt and Road may fully coordinate their economic development strategies and policies.

There are three levels of coordination. First, to jointly build the Belt and Road Initiative, Chinese government abandoned the idea that the coordination means you accept China's plan or vice versa and stresses finding common grounds and cooperation fields on the basis of mutual respect and then jointly make plans. Second, it is designed to coordinate development strategies among the countries. For example, many development strategies in India can coordinate with the 21st Century Maritime Silk Road, such as the Project Mausam proposed by Modi administration which is aimed at reviving the cultural exchanges between the ancient sea lanes in India and countries along the Indian Ocean. The third is the coordination between projects and enterprises. Many countries along the Belt and Road are developing port infrastructure, shipping industry, fishing industry and fishing products processing industry, planning port neighboring industrial parks, special zones, bonded zones and FTAs. There are many similar projects and all these enjoy market potential. Many non-governmental organizations are establishing bridges for enterprises, and state governments are protecting their enterprises. They help enterprises to conduct project cooperation, tap complementary advantages, shoulder risks and share benefits.

Fourth, from cooperation mechanisms, the main target is to jointly build the 'Belt and Road' mechanism. In this regard, the Initiative can borrow the existing bilateral and multilateral cooperation mechanisms and platforms, for example, the Shanghai Cooperation Organization (SCO), ASEAN Plus China (10+1), Asia-Pacific Economic Cooperation (APEC), Asia-Europe Meeting (ASEM), Asia Cooperation Dialogue (ACD), Conference on Interaction and Confidence-Building Measures in Asia (CICA), China-Arab States Cooperation Forum (CASCF), China-Gulf Cooperation Council Strategic Dialogue, Greater Mekong Sub-region (GMS) Economic Cooperation, and Central Asia Regional Economic Cooperation (CAREC) to attract more countries and regions to participate in the 'Belt and Road' Initiative. Meanwhile, efforts should be made to launch new bilateral and multilateral mechanisms and platforms and China welcomes the participation of the countries along the road to contribute new thinking.

In conclusion, the Belt and Road Initiative proposed by the Chinese government has transparent policies and did not include any conspiracy.

Is OBOR squeezing India's development space?

From geographic location, India is located on the south section (the Road) and the north sections (One Belt) are countries and regions surrounding India. This geo-political pattern enables people to imagine whether India's strategic space will be squeezed by the Belt and Road Initiative. We need to consider this issue from the following perspectives.

- Community of Shared Interests,

- Community of Shared Destiny and

- Community of Shared Responsibility

The Vision and the Actions advocates to jointly build the 'Belt and Road' Initiative with relevant countries to promote practical cooperation in all fields, and works to build a community of shared interests, destiny and responsibility featuring mutual political trust, economic integration and cultural inclusiveness. The principle of building a community of shared interests, destiny and responsibility shows that China does not have the intention to squeeze the strategic space of India.

China and India have undeniable historical conflicts. In particular, the 1962 War, the territorial disputes and the so called "Tibetan Issue" between China and India have caused many negative influences on the development of the healthy relationship between China and India. It is also the origin of hostility among the two peoples. Facing the reality, if the two countries focus on the historical conflicts and pay attention to the factors constraining the bilateral relationship and do not establish a community of shared interests featuring mutual benefit and win-win results, it will be detrimental to the long term relationship and overall interests of the two countries. From this perspective, the construction of the Belt and Road Initiative focuses on the establishment of the community of shared interests.

For the community of shared destiny that Chinese government stresses, it involves a reliable support, energy and resources guarantee and a network of international exchange, and aims at extending China's period of strategic opportunity. China and India are both big countries of real economy and developing countries. The history and reality show China and India have a shared destiny and China hopes to form a closer community of shared destiny with India and other countries along the Belt and Road.

At the same time, on the basis of establishing a community of shared interests featuring mutual benefit and win-win results and a community of shared destiny featuring common development and prosperity, China and India should shoulder common responsibilities. The Vision and the Actions stresses that China is committed to shouldering more responsibilities and obligations within its capabilities.

OBOR initiatives respects the differences among countries

The Vision and the Actions states that The 'Belt and Road' Initiative is in line with the purposes and principles of the UN Charter; it upholds the "Five Principles of Peaceful Coexistence: mutual respect for each other's sovereignty and territorial integrity, mutual non-aggression, mutual non-interference in each other's internal affairs, equality and mutual benefit, and peaceful coexistence" and it thinks that this is the political prerequisite for participating in the Belt and Road Initiative. On this basis, the Vision and the Actions also elaborates that the initiative needs the principle of harmony, inclusiveness, and tolerance among civilizations. In the process of establishing the Belt and Road Initiative, China does not stress that other countries should follow China's development path and model and that China wants to destroy the cultures and civilizations of other countries, instead, China will respect the choices of development paths and models by other countries and supports dialogues among different civilizations on the principles of seeking common ground while shelving differences and drawing on each other's strengths, so that all countries can coexist in peace for common prosperity.

China and India are both ancient civilizations and enjoy their own development paths and patterns. The aim of elaborating on respecting the differences of different countries is to realize common prosperity between China and India in the process of development, not to set a framework for China to squeeze India's strategic space.

OBOR hold a right perspective of the competition between China and India

Competition and cooperation are common phenomenon and rule in the economic field. In the process of jointly building the Belt and Road Initiative, cooperation and competition co-exist. Only cooperation can realize win-win results and multi-win and only competition can improve efficiency. There must be a scenario in the real world: there will be more cooperation and more competition between China and India. In fact, before the OBOR initiative was proposed, China and countries along the Belt and Road Initiative have maintained friendly relationship and close communications and cooperation both in trade and people to people contact. Exporting resources into the region and forming competition in the economic and trade aspects is not a result of the Belt and Road Initiative.

It is found through analysis that in the Initiative, competition mainly appears in the economic and trade fields instead of other fields. In the past, China is a traditional world factory and a big manufacturing country and India is a traditional world office and a big service country. However, from the current and future development trend, China is also building high-end service industry and India is trying great efforts to reconstruct its manufacturing basis. China and India enjoy competition and cooperation at the same time and there is even greater cooperation than competition.

The Maritime Silk Road in the history was a maritime trade network among the ports between the East Asia and the east coast of Africa. It started from Quanzhou and went across Southeast Asia, India and the Arabian Peninsula. It established a high degree of prosperity from the late Tang Dynasty and Song Dynasty, promoted the spread of trade, geographic knowledge and navigation technology. In ancient times, this is the proof of the peaceful and friendly relations between China, South Asia and Southeast Asia and also reflects that China attached importance to the harmonious relationship with neighbouring countries and equal trade exchanges. This is completely different from the colonialist practice of Europe. Deeply impacted by colonialism, China and India are both Asian countries, and China can understand India's vigilance towards China in opening up the maritime trading route.

It should be seen that the sound competition under the prerequisite of cooperation will have a positive influence on the region. There is a golden rule in economics: lack of competition results in lack of efficiency and the competition under the prerequisite of cooperation is beneficial for improving economic vitality and the rapid and healthy development of participating economy. China stresses that it has both cooperation and competition with countries along the 'Belt and Road' but it is necessary to avoid vicious competition. China and India conducting competition on the basis of cooperation are conducive to both sides and not to squeezing India's strategic space.

China will not monopolize the benefits of the Belt and Road Initiative

The reason for proposing the Initiative for China is to tap the specific values and the ideas of the ancient Silk Road, i.e. conduct mutual learning and draw from the strength of each other so as to inject new contents in the new era and realize common development and common prosperity in the region and in the neighbouring countries. This is a cooperative initiative and idea and will help the countries along the Belt and Road to conduct all kinds of cooperation, in particular the connectivity cooperation in the Silk Road spirit. In this way, the cooperation will be mutually reinforcing and thus accelerate the development of the countries.

Furthermore, the Vision and the Actions also elaborates the idea of opening up and cooperate and also stated that the countries along the Belt and Road Initiative are within but not limited to the ancient Silk Road scope. Countries, international and regional organizations can also participate to bring the achievements to wider regions. The inclusiveness of the Belt and Road Initiative will remove people's worries about China monopolizing the benefits of the Belt and Road Initiative and completely dismiss the myth of China squeezing India's strategy.

OBOR Economic Corridors

Bangladesh-China-India-Myanmar (BCIM) Economic Corridor

The BCIM Economic Corridor initiative was proposed by Prime Minister Li Keqiang when he was visiting India in May, 2013. The Joint Statement between the People's Republic of China and the Republic of India officially proposed the establishment of the BCIM Economic Corridor, which received positive response from Bangladesh and Myanmar. On June 9th, 2014, the Prime Minister of Bangladesh, Dr. Sheikh Hasina noted in Beijing that the development of Bangladesh needs BCIM Economic Corridor and it is very important for Bangladesh. Meanwhile, the development of BCIM will become part of the Silk Road Economic Belt and Maritime Silk Road. In 2014, the trade volume between China and India, Bangladesh and Myanmar exceeds one quarter of China's total trade, accounting for 26.7%. The growth rate of the import and export in the countries of the Trans-Himalayan region reached 25.8%, higher than the national average.[4]

Premier Li Keqiang's proposal was formerly named BCIM Regional Economic Cooperation, which was proposed in the late 1990s by scholars from Yunnan province in China and was well received by India, Myanmar and Bangladesh. In 1999, the first Forum on Regional Cooperation among Bangladesh, China, India and Myanmar was firstly held in Kunming and was then held 11 times since. In 2011, Yunnan Academy of Social Sciences officially proposed the vision of BCIM-Kunming-Mandalay-Dacca-Calcutta Economic Corridor. BCIM Economic Corridor had an early start as an important part of the 'Belt and Road', Initiative and laid a solid foundation for the smooth implementation of the Belt and Road Initiative.

China-Pakistan Economic Corridor (CPEC)

China-Pakistan Economic Corridor was proposed by Premier Li Keqiang when he was visiting Pakistan in May, 2013. The initial aim of the strategy was to enhance the exchange and cooperation between China and Pakistan in the field of transportation, energy, strengthen connectivity and promote common development. The corridor begins with Kashgar and ends with Gwadar in Pakistan with a total distance of 3000 kilometers.[5] It connects with the Silk Road Economic Belt in the north, 21st Century Maritime Silk Road in the south and serves as a crucial hub.[6] It is a trade corridor which includes highway, railway, oil and natural gas as well as optical cable channel and it is an important part of the 'Belt and Road' Initiative.[7]

China-Pakistan Economic Corridor is planned to start from Gwadar, go all the way to the north to cross Pakistan and connect Xinjiang Uighur Autonomous Region through railway and highway. Once it is completed, China will not have to travel through the Indian Ocean and the Malacca Strait to import the crude oil and cargo from the Middle East and ship back the goods from the South China Sea. The goods can get on aboard at the Gwadar port and can be transported to China through the economic corridor. It will save two thirds of the distance and will reduce relevant risks. The reality, however, is far from it. Shipping oil and other goods through the economic corridor by railway and highway will cost 4 times higher than through the Malacca Strait, so it is not cost effective. Inferred from the Gravity Model of Economics, the volume of goods transported can cover the odds of the daily operating costs.[8]

However, China-Pakistan Economic Corridor goes across the Kashmir region which is controlled by Pakistan, so India has grave concerns over this, as this might be used for military purpose by China and Pakistan.[9]

China-India Economic Corridor

In May, 2015, when Indian Prime Minister Narenda Modi visited China, Chinese leaders proposed to establish China-India Economic Corridor, build a railway across Tibet and connect three countries and carry out a series of major projects to help Nepal with post-disaster construction. From China's perspective, the idea of establishing China-India Economic Corridor is to mainly help Nepal to carry out post-disaster construction and play the role of a responsible big neighbour. Secondly, another important consideration of this idea is to promote connectivity among Tibet, Nepal and India. For Nepal, a country that regards tourism as a major pillar industry, the construction of China-India Economic Corridor will help to improve Nepal's domestic transportation infrastructure and thus attract more Chinese tourists to Nepal.

Trans-Himalayan Economic Zone of Cooperation

In January, 2015, The Report on the Work of the Tibet's Autonomous Region Government proposed to further expand domestic and external opening up, co-construct the Trans-Himalayan Economic Zone of Cooperation and take the initiative to connect with the Belt and Road Initiative and BCIM Economic Corridor. The Trans-Himalayan Economic Zone of Cooperation in a narrow sense refers to Khasa, Gyirong and Purang County as windows, Lhasa and Shigatse as interior support and develops border trade, international tourism, Tibetan medicine industry, special agriculture and grassland farming and cultural industry with Nepal, India, Bhutan and Bangladesh as markets. The Trans-Himalayan Economic Zone of Cooperation in a broad sense refers to expanding the Trans-Himalayan Economic Zone of Cooperation to South Asia and Southeast Asia with BCIM as the core. The Vision and the actions does not specify this concept and only mentioned the idea of promoting the border trade and tourism and cultural cooperation between Tibetan Autonomous Region and neighboring countries

Does the Belt and Road Initiative challenges Trans-Pacific Partnership (TPP)?

On February 4th, 2016, 12 member countries of the Trans-Pacific Partnership (TPP) Agreement officially singed the agreement in Auckland, Newzealand. The feature of this organization is to cover tariff (mutual exemption of tariff involving over 10000 commodities), investment, and competition policies, technological and trade barriers, food safety, intellectual property, government procurement, green development and labor protection and so on. The US has been excluding China in regional economic cooperation such as TPP, so some domestic think tanks in China regard TPP as an economic NATO. Some people speculate that China wants to use the Belt and Road Initiative against TPP. Some Indian scholars think that India should make a choice between TPP and the Belt and Road Initiative.

As far as I am concerned, the Belt and Road Initiative should be understood under the overall framework of China's diplomatic policies and security strategies.

Firstly, China's domestic affairs and diplomatic relationship. A country always handles diplomacy from the perspective of domestic affairs and diplomacy is an extension of the domestic affairs. The former always serves the latter. China's biggest domestic affair today is China's modernization. China proposed the Four Modernizations (modernization of agriculture, industry, national defence and science and technology) in the 1980s. Chinese president Xi Jinping proposed "Two Hundred Year Dreams" (the first is to build a moderately well-off society in all round aspects at the 100thanniversary of the establishment of Communist party of China (CPC); the second is to build a prosperous, democratic, civilized and harmonious socialist modern country at the 100th anniversary of the founding of China. Currently, the biggest problem facing China's domestic affairs is to accelerate its own development, i.e. realizing sustainable and rapid economic development to build China into a moderately developed country, and solve the poverty alleviation issue of 100 million people in central and western China to enable them to live good live. China formulated the Belt and Road Initiative from the perspective of its domestic affairs, i.e. solve urgent problems based on the reality.

Secondly, China's foreign policy, since 1982, has been adhering to the Independent Foreign Policy of Peace featuring no alliance and no dependency so as to strive for a peaceful environment and promote world peace. China holds the foreign policy of "great powers as the key, neighbor countries take the first priority, developing countries as the base and multilateral diplomacy as the stage." The 'Belt and Road' Initiative should follow this foreign policy

Thirdly, China's Asian Policies. For a long term, China has been adhering to the Asian foreign policy of "building friendship and partnership with neighboring countries, and pursuing the policy of bringing harmony, security and prosperity to neighbors". India is a big country, a neighbor, a developing country and an emerging economy, so it is an important aspect of China's diplomacy and Asian policies. The Belt and Road Initiative needs India's support and this will also benefit India.

Fourthly, Chinese government made it clear that China's development policy is not to seek hegemony, rather identified the path of peaceful rise and adopted the attitudes of no challenge to, participation in and promotion of the existing world system. The existing world system features a political system with the UN as the core, a financial system with IMF/World Bank and settlement using US dollars as the center and a trading system with WTO at the core. China's proposal of the 'Belt and Road' Initiative is not a challenge to the existing world system. Under this prerequisite, the establishment of this Initiative did not rebuild the international monetary system nor held the intention of changing international trade rules. Judging from the future trend, the RMB will be chosen with the construction of the Belt and Road Initiative and it will be chosen along with China's cooperation with other countries, It is worth noting that RMB is not the only official currency in the Belt and Road Initiative. It is inevitable that new rules will appear in the trade and investment negotiation. It is only a supplement and improvement to the current international economic and financial order and will not replace nor could replace the practicing international trade rules.

Placing the 'Belt and Road' Initiative under the background of Chinese foreign policy and security strategy clearly suggests that the 'Belt and Road' Initiative will not challenge TPP. The US excluding China in TPP means that it will exclude China thereafter. China not participating in TPP does not mean China will not have this option in the future one should not place TPP and OBOR against each other or regard them as two political groups and chooses sides.

Conclusion

Asia's future lies in India and China. A famous Indian poet once said that "China and India are brothers". It not only applies to the past but also to the future. Asia and the world is big enough to host China and India at the same time and both the Countries can go hand in hand for future development. India is a big Asian country that enjoys robust development momentum. It is possible to reduce misunderstandings and coordinate India's domestic actions and plans with the Belt and Road Initiative proposed by China so that the two close brothers in ancient times can hold hands together in the new Asia too in the 21st century.

End Notes

1   http://finance.ifeng.com/news/people/20121016/7154995.shtml

2   张智：《一带一路加速亚太互连互通中国版马歇尔计划启航，《华夏日报》2014年11月8日 ZHANG Zhi: The Belt and Road Initiative accelerates Asia-Pacific connectivity, China's Marshall Plan Launches, *Huaxia Daily*, November 8th,2014

3   经济日报/2015 年/6 月/17 日/第004 版 Economic Daily;June 17th,2015;004 Edition

4   http://www.chinabond.com.cn/Info/20139645

5   中巴经济走廊建设成为新疆发展强大引擎．中国日报．2015-04-24 [引用日期 2015-04-25] The Construction of China-Pakistan Economic Corridor Becomes Huge Engine for Xinjiang's Development; China Daily; April 24, 2015

6   中巴经济走廊："一带一路"推进的"示范区"（组图）．网易．2015-04-19 [引用日期2015-04-25] China-Pakistan Economic Corridor: The Demonstration Zone of the Belt and Road Initiative, Netease; April 19th, 2015

7   中巴经济走廊建设成为新疆发展强大引擎．中国日报．2015-04-24 [引用日期2015-04-25]．The Construction of China-Pakistan Economic Corridor Becomes Huge Engine for Xinjiang's Development; China Daily; April 24, 2015

8   See http://bbs.tianya.cn/post-worldlook-1452277-1.shtml

9   See http://finance.ifeng.com/a/20150603/13751733_0.shtml

2

China-India in the Context of One Belt One Road: Divergences and Concerns

Huang Yunsong

The One Belt One Road initiative (hereinafter referred to as OBOR) proposed by Chinese leadership in late 2013 boasts of great aspiration for prosperity and development not only for China itself, but also for all the states along the route. The lofty initiative obviously cannot be materialized, if there are any inimical connotations or potential threats in direct sense to either peace or sustainable benefits of the states involved, despite of the high-profile promotions by the Chinese governmental agencies and its business community at various international and national forums. After substantial exchanges and communications with the experts and intellectuals from both China and India, it is found that the major hurdles preventing the initiative from meaningful fruition are so complex and diversified, ranging from geopolitical implications, security concerns, differences in development patterns, etc.

It is quite true that the Chinese leadership and the strategic community hasn't given adequate attention to these pertinent matters, and more efforts were needed to address the concerns of the states yet to physically participate in the OBOR initiative, which contributes to the bifurcation in the interpretation of the OBOR, or even overt rejection by certain states. Therefore, a well understanding of the divergences and concerns related to the essentially unilateral proposal, and a proactive effort in narrowing the gap of perception is indispensable for both China and India, in order to steer away from further confrontations due to various Silk Road projects in India's periphery in the worst sense, or to enable the two parties to join hands for the OBOR venture in the best sense. It is also quite necessary to examine at macro-level on OBOR's possible impact upon the existing world order, and at micro-level on some issues such as CPEC, India's oil exploration in South China Sea, in addition to the frequently visited historical topics such as the border dispute and China-Pakistan relations, bearing in mind that the reasons leading to India's current detachment from the OBOR must be multifold.

Maritime Silk Road: India's Contact Point to OBOR

The OBOR runs from East Asia to Europe through land route and maritime route. In light of *Vision and Actions on Jointly Building Silk Road Economic Belt and 21st-Century Maritime Silk Road*, the most authoritative literature about the OBOR released by the Chinese Government in 28 March 2015, some Chinese scholars strongly believe that **South Asia factors primarily on the Maritime Silk Road (MSR)**, and its role in the Silk Road Economic Belt (SREB) is at best marginal, though the SREB is also designed to connect China with Southeast Asia, **South Asia** and the Indian Ocean. Against this backdrop, it is very understandable that in most cases the debates on the OBOR within the Indian strategic community are focused on the MSR.

By reading between the lines of the OBOR initiative, it can be found that the MSR blueprint is actually a product by upgrading and expanding the China-ASEAN trade and economic cooperation, which has experienced a glorious decade of rapid development since the strategic partnership between the two was established in 2003.[1] When China became the largest trading partner of ASEAN, and ASEAN the third largest trading partner of China in 2010 with facilitation of the free trade mechanism, the bilateral relations started to bear fruit on political, social and cultural fronts, substantially enhancing the values and strategic security of maritime trading routes. Both China and ASEAN have benefited significantly from the remarkable surge of the bilateral trade as a confidence-building measure that persists in the face of the critical political relations due to the disputes in the South China Sea. Perceived as a helpful model of economic means for safety goals, an upgraded version of the maritime trading scheme, known as the 21st-Century Maritime Silk Road, is also considered appropriate for South Asia by the Chinese leadership.

The Indian subcontinent, protruding into the Indian Ocean on the south, and flanked by the Arabian Sea on the west, and the Bay of Bengal on the east, sits right at one of the most important junctures along the MSR. It is not only capable of facilitating MSR's connectivity endeavors, but also can be equipped to strangle China's outreach to west Asia, east Africa and Europe. However, China cautiously chose to look at the bright side of picture. In addition to the subcontinent's key geographical position in the context of the MSR, over 24% of the world's population, a vast array of youth workforce,[2]and the great potential of an unsaturated economy also provide China with great opportunities for trade and investment. To a great extent, the economic growth of China depends on the subcontinent more than Europe, the nominal destination of the OBOR. Therefore, China is determined to achieve all-around cooperation with this piece of land in terms of connectivity, trade, financial integration and people-to-people bond.

Undoubtedly, the subcontinent's role in the MSR can be much greater than a mere transit stop, and the MSR's materialization also heavily relies on the active participation of the subcontinent states. As the predominant player in South Asia and an emerging power in the world arena, India maintains the decisive influence upon its South Asian neighbors, especially Sri Lanka, Nepal and Maldives, though its relations with them are occasionally tense and bumpy. Recognizing India's unique political and economic status, Beijing has made a pragmatic move to invite Delhi to join the OBOR, so as to secure the smooth implementation of Maritime Silk Road projects within and beyond the subcontinent, as well as the Indian Ocean Region. India, well aware of China's ambition and enthusiasm for overseas development, is still looking at the MSR with a contradictory mentality, trying hard to balance between its thirst for infrastructural renovation and industrial capacity and its long-standing strategic goal to curtail the expansion of China's charisma both at the regional and global level, and digging deep for clues to China's strategic conspiracy to justify its suspicion and repulsion in the MSR.

An Over Interpretation

According to the official statistics,[3] India dropped out of the Top Ten trading partners list of China in 2014, indicating the chill crawling into their economic engagement. The bilateral trade, missing the target of USD 100 billion by 2015 set by the Chinese Government, has stalled after the encouraging rapid growth till 2011, fluctuating at the level of USD 70 billion for half a decade.[4]Although the real bilateral trade between the two, as predicted by a prominent Indian economic expert, is actually six to eight times the size shown by statistics on the paper,[5] China has been worried about the stagnation and the striking imbalance of bilateral economic and trade relations with India, and its ominous meaning for their fragile political tranquility. Since China and India are considerably more reliant on each other than public recognition at the economic front, and provides a solid basis for peace and prosperity in the center of Asia, the OBOR at this point can become a realistic solution to further the bond between the two Asian powers by making use of China's industrial overcapacity and investment to facilitate PM Modi's program of "Make in India". It seems, however, that the understanding of the two sides in the mammoth initiative of OBOR differs enormously for its long-term prospects to their geo-political relations. The empirical formula proven largely viable in the China-ASEAN interaction has encountered an implied rejection in South Asia, and its direct cause is rather geo-strategic than economic, as well as the centrality pattern of power structure within the region, which is extremely different from that of ASEAN.

The OBOR is believed to have an important effect on the region's economic architecture – patterns of regional trade, investment, infrastructure development – and in turn strategic implications for China, the United States, and other major powers (including India).[6]By downplaying China's well intention and win-win potential of the initiative, some strategic advisors repeatedly reminded Delhi of the risk that the OBOR, particularly the MSR will heighten geopolitical tensions in the Indian Ocean Region, exaggerating the security concern of the likely expansion of China's naval power abroad. Ironically, a textual examination of the OBOR official document authorized by China State Council clearly reveals that the OBOR is actually pursuing complete non-confrontational approach, which in nature is an economic and trade promotion centric plan, focusing on cooperation and development in a joint manner.

Firstly, feeling threatened by China's naval activities in the Indian Ocean, and its port construction projects in other South Asian countries like Pakistan, Sri Lanka and Bangladesh, the India Government has apparently bought the speculation that the MSR, taken as an alternative term of the "String of Pearls", will pave the way for China's military encirclement of India. Secondly, the China-Pakistan Economic Corridor (CPEC) and the Bangladesh-China-India-Myanmar Economic Corridor (BCIM),only closely related to the OBOR but wrongly considered by the Indian strategic community as its integral parts, also add up to India's suspicion that China will clandestinely tackle with its war-torn west flank in Kashmir and the rebellious territory in the Northeast. Thirdly, Chinese OBOR initiative was also deemed by some Indian experts as the response to the US Pivot to Asia policy, pointing towards an "alternative world order" that is being shaped with Asia at the center.[7] Unfortunately, India was quickly overwhelmed by the OBOR's overemphasis on the infrastructure projects and their military potential, before it could give a thorough consideration to the dynamics in the east hemisphere. By turning a cold shoulder to the BCIM, launching strong protests towards China over the CPEC, and vigorously dislodging Sri Lanka from the first rank to implement the OBOR port projects, India has sent a clear message to China that the OBOR has not been well received for its ambiguous strategic implications, and the MSR doesn't justify the increasing presence of Chinese navy in the Indian Ocean.

OBOR's Zeal and Failure in Infrastructure Projects in India

With the help of the Asian Infrastructure Investment Bank (AIIB), the Chinese Government is committed to invest USD 3.8 trillion into infrastructures and other facilities in the developing countries along the OBOR land and maritime routes. Taking rate of return into consideration, infrastructures can be the least cost-effective investment that China can think of, especially in the regions where it had a history of failure. As estimated by some Chinese economic experts, the infrastructure investments that China did in Africa in the 1970s generated no return at all. However, according to the relevant studies, infrastructure investments, in transportation for example, have long term economic benefits: firstly, large private sector productivity gains from infrastructure investments, stimulating economic growth, productivity, and land values, etc.; secondly, investing in infrastructure creates jobs in the construction, manufacturing, and retail sectors; thirdly, investing in infrastructure uses underutilized resources and considerably reduces unemployment rate; fourthly, the gap of USD 800 billion between the supply and demand for infrastructure spending in Asia will mostly be filled, leading to more sustainable and inclusive growth. During the emerging-market frenzy from 2003 to 2010, it was the western multinationals that poured USD 2 trillion into facilities and factories in places like China and India. Now it seems to be an optimal time for China to take the lead in infrastructure investment in the 44 states along the OBOR routes into high speed railways, deep water ports, and highway networks, which will provide ample opportunities for the Chinese public and private sectors to capitalize on. But China's drive for success in infrastructure investment on the subcontinent was choked.

India's ruling party Bharatiya Janata Party (BJP) firstly announced the Diamond Quadrilateral high speed rail project connecting Chennai, Delhi, Kolkata and Mumbai announced in its Election Manifesto in early 2014, then there came another great news for foreign investors like China and Japan that the Modi Administration finally allowed 100% foreign direct investment in railways infrastructure in mid-2014, which previously was not allowed in this sector at all. In November 2015, the Indian Government took a fresh set of measures to ease foreign direct investment restrictions to allow more foreign funds into protected sectors. However, with a series of failure in their bids for infrastructure projects in India and in its periphery, the exciting news has become increasingly irrelevant to the Chinese investors and manufacturers, and some of them grew less confident that they are welcomed on this part of the subcontinent. Broadly speaking, the difficulty of doing business in India does not bother Chinese entrepreneurs that much.[8] Moreover, the stringent labor laws, the land acquisition laws and the complex domestic tax regime make no difference between the foreign investors. When India sealed USD 12 Billion high-speed rail deal with Japan in December 2015,[9] regardless of the cost advantage of the deal offered by China, it is evident that India is using the infrastructure projects as a diplomatic tool to prevent the OBOR initiative from expanding China's presence in the region. Given the past difficulties in implementing the OBOR, China has to give its zeal for the infrastructure projects in India and in its periphery a serious reassessment. Similarly, the risks of China's infrastructure investments in other South Asia states like Sri Lank will remain until a comprehensive understanding is reached between China and India.

Debates on the Difference in Development Patterns

Apart from the ominous strategic implications, the OBOR initiative was also criticized by some Indian scholars on the basis of the development pattern it represents, which was doubted as incompatible to the social and political reality in India. Firstly, the OBOR initiative anticipates possible policy convergence in the aspect of development patterns between China and other sovereign national governments along the routes, without giving adequate attentions to the social and political actors within these states, especially at sub-national levels, and their possible responses and motivations as decisive factors, which in turn manifests the divergence over development aspirations. In the most recent case of BJP's loss in Bihar elections, despite the lucrative infrastructure package for developing rural roads, highways, village electrification, and railway capacity that Prime Minister Modi promised Bihar population, he could not win the hearts of the Behari people and win the election there, hence, the argument that a development program if not carefully calibrated then will not last for long has been proven valid. Secondly, it was suggested that the OBOR initiative is not a need based development pattern where local social actors aspires for a road, bridge or a factory as means to improve living standards. Driven by the substantial production capability of some state owned enterprises, the OBOR initiative is advocating on the subcontinent a capacity based development aspirations that could lead to a disastrous social outcome and therefore can produce different responses from local social constituencies. Besides, the specific legal norms and compliance standards will also need a substantial period of time for the OBOR initiative to be localized in the states along the routes.[10]

As a matter of fact, the above arguments, criticizing the OBOR's lack of inclusiveness and attention to the need of interested or affected states along the routes, were not an entirely objective evaluation. The Modi administration has decided about the industrial capacity matters desperately needed in India, while how to achieve the capacity in an optimized manner by factoring the social and political needs at the sub-national levels is basically another issue that does not contradict the need itself. The ambitious "Make in India" program to transform India into a global manufacturing powerhouse – a China dominant field for the past three decades –is aimed to attract fresh foreign investment and spur job creation. It was the answer that the Modi Administration delivered to Indian voters based on its reading of their needs. According to Raja Mohan, India badly needs connectivity in its frontier, coastal and hinterland areas,[11] which is exactly a connectivity-centric plan like the OBOR pledges to provide for industrial capacity transfer. Although the debate on the development patterns provides good food for thought, and China has shown great sincerity to improve OBOR's inclusiveness through bilateral mechanism, the lynchpin in fact rests on India's will to partner with China.

China's Presence in the Indian Ocean Region

China's economic and naval presence in the Indian Ocean Region is not as confrontational as some Indian strategists predicts. Firstly, China's presence in the Indian Ocean Region is benign in nature, and closely connected to its overseas economic efforts. Taking Chinese-African trade relations for example, with the bilateral trade soaring to over $200 billion and its direct investment in Africa increasing by nearly 50 percent annually, China has become the largest trading partner of the poorest continent since 2009.[12] Hoping to keep the momentum in developing the economic ties with Africa and other states in the IOR, China has committed itself to infrastructure upgrade along the maritime trade route, by bringing in investments in port facilities in a number of IOR states, and exploring opportunities in Maldives, the Seychelles, and Mauritius. In the OBOR initiative, China regards India is as one of the major partners, hoping to release the great potential in their bilateral economic relations. Unfortunately, China's economic initiatives have been seriously misinterpreted by the strategic community in India, saying it is economic means for military ends. If any civilian facilities are supposed be categorized as military just because they can be used for military purpose in one way or another, then the rationale of the above argument is absolutely unbeatable, and the distinction between the civilian and military facilities becomes pointless.

Secondly, China's naval presence is marginal and capable of no threat to the IOR. The Chinese naval presence in the Indian Ocean, especially in the Arabian Sea, is not even commensurate to its huge economic and strategic interests in place. China's naval strength is and will continue to be bound in the South and East China Sea, focusing on defending sovereignty rights over Taiwan, the Diaoyu islands, and the maritime interests related to certain land features. The strongest foreign military presence in the IOR is maintained by the US. The Indian Ocean is the operating area of its 5th, 6th and 7th fleets. The 5th, reactivated in 1995, is a fully Indian Ocean fleet, and comprised of a carrier strike group, amphibious ready group, and a number of other ships and aircrafts, with 15,000 personnel serving afloat and 1,000 ashore. In addition, there are around 5,000 troops living in the US military base on Diego Garcia. Except for its supremacy in the Arabian Sea and the Bay of Bengal, India has also nurtured its military presence in at least 8 foreign states, including the surveillance installations in Madagascar, Mauritius and Seychelles, capable of exercising meaningful influence over various choke points around the Indian Ocean to secure the sea lanes, especially the Strait of Malacca. Since December 2008, with the authorization from the UN Security Council, China has dispatched 21 Escort Task Groups to the Indian Ocean to repress piracy and respond to humanitarian crisis in the region. In addition to counter-piracy patrols, the Task Groups also conducted missions to escort cargo ships carrying chemical weapons out of Syria, and provide search and rescue support for Malaysia Airlines MH370. Among these 63 Chinese naval ships of the task groups, half of them belong to the South Sea Fleet, and the total number of the sailors in each Task Group is usually around 800. Has anyone asked the question, why South Sea Fleet? The purpose of its heavy involvement in the missions is to avail them the training opportunities for low intensity combat proficiency, an obvious response to the tensions in South China Sea.

Thirdly, China's naval presence is on ad hoc basis. As Chinese military experts pointing out, China's Escort Task Groups operating in the Indian Ocean are very different from a regular naval deployment, and legitimacy of their operation largely relies on the renewal of the relevant UNSC resolution. In other words, there must be some very good reasons, if Chinese navy decides to stay in the Indian Ocean when the threat from piracy and terrorism is no more. The thriller stories of Chinese ghost fleet and the String of Pearls, focusing on China's military appetite in the Indian Ocean, have been developed into something unreal, without the least respect for the fact that there is almost no diplomatically reliable, logistically functional and militarily defendable strategic foothold for China's naval force in this region. Since the low level presence of Chinese navy in the IOR works perfectly well to keep our cargo ships and tankers free of pirate harassment, and guarantees that the chance of escalated confrontation held in check, there is no necessity for China to resort to a regular naval deployment in the near future. Similarly, the so called string of pearls consisting of multiple naval bases along the rim of the Indian Ocean is not only be too luxurious for China to afford, but also incompatible to China's capability and aspiration. This is why Chinese strategic community usually takes this hypothesis not so seriously. It is true that Chinese government has funded the majority of the $1.2 billion construction in Gwadar, but independent media such as Economist has found the port facility project to be commercial in nature. The berth rights and logistic support possibly available to China's naval vessels doesn't automatically turn Gwadar into a military base comparable to Diego Garcia.

Fourthly, China is in favor of a collective security mechanism in the Indian Ocean Region, which is supposed to be inclusive to all stakeholders. China's security concept does not support division of spheres of influence, or advocate for the notions such as strategic backyard. For the past three decades, this security concept has influenced China's foreign policies very deeply, and helped in achieving better relations with ASEAN, formation of the SCO, and the joint efforts with the U.S. in control of nuclear proliferation in North Korea and Iran. In order to secure its overseas interests, China has to be pragmatic enough to depend on various collective security mechanisms around the world. This established approach pursued by China allows little room for hegemon or monopoly on security matters in specific regions. It is also true that foreign military bases are not prerequisite for the collective security mechanism to work. More intriguingly, in regard to India's renewed enthusiasm in promoting the Indian Ocean as a Zone of Peace, it is believed that Beijing will stand firmly for New Delhi, if the suggestion of no military bases in the Indian Ocean region (IOR) is for all the major powers including the US. Would also like to mention that during the Ad-hoc Committee meeting in July 2005, the Chinese representative did call for the major powers outside the region, to eliminate their military bases in the IOR. When security of the IOR comes into question, China sincerely encourages the relevant parties to consider and respect China's well-grounded concern for the safety of its economic activities and crucial trading routes, by assuming an objective attitude in telling the difference between presence and threat, the distinction between commercial ports and military bases. China is willing and capable of being a net provider of security to the IOR, as long as it is not excluded from the collective security mechanism yet to emerge.

Complexity in the South China Sea

Sea lines of communication are closely related to national security and prosperity of all states, that any attempts to disrupt international shipping lanes should not be tolerated by the world community. Chinese government has reiterated at various international forums its position on safeguarding and ensuring freedom of navigation and over flight throughout the region, especially in the South China Sea. Over 100,000 vessels sail through the South China Sea every year, their freedom of navigation has not been interrupted. For almost half of India's external trade that passes through the South China Sea, there has never been any issue with the freedom of navigation. The so-called issue of navigation freedom being endangered in the South China Sea and the militarization in the region is actually a pseudo-proposition. India's indirect involvement into the disputes in the South China Sea not only increases its political frictions with China, but also makes it even more difficult for both to cultivate close relationship.

Because of the cruise by the US'S Curtis Wilbur sailing within 12 nautical miles of Triton Island, USS Lassen within 12 nautical miles of and Subi Reef, and the US bombers closely flying by, the situation in the South China Sea is seemingly approaching to a breaking point. The cruise and over flight was perceived by Chinese government as escalatory and provocative, because they were meant to exert undue pressure on China alone, and encourage the relevant states to take a tougher stance in negotiations for solution. When China is fully aware that these activities around its artificial islands are not in violation of international law, it has become pointless and counter-productive for the US or its intimate partner states to carry on with the operation. It's unwise for the US to be obsessed with threat of force when dealing with China, if it really wants both parties to have enough room to maneuver.

Since India, along with a few other states, has publicly voiced its support for freedom of navigation in international waters, including the South China Sea, it is really necessary to focus the attention on the different interpretation of UNCLOS concerning the freedom of navigation. After careful examination of relevant legal documents, it is found that India's perception of the freedom of navigation is virtually very similar to that of China, which rules out the foreign military activities in its exclusive economic zone. As per the Declaration made upon ratification of UNCLOS by India on June 29, 1995, the second paragraph reads as, "The Government of the Republic of India understands that the provisions of the convention do not authorize other States to carry out in the exclusive economic zone and on the continental shelf military exercises or maneuvers, in particular those involving the use of weapons or explosives without the consent of the coastal State."

In addition to China and India, 26 states (including Vietnam) have also put restrictions on foreign military activities according to their interpretation of the UNCLOS. In this sense, international law (including the UNCLOS) does not provide the United States with the navigational freedom as it claims. The other thing that needs to be stressed is that the

UNCLOS doesn't prohibit signatory parties from the activities of land reclamation. If the US wants to play judge on whether China, Vietnam or Philippine has been excessive in land reclamation and claiming maritime interests, then US must earn the ticket by ratifying the UNCLOS first. Because the UNCLOS is not simply a forum for any bystanders, but a legal regime for parties committed to it. In all, the confrontation between the U.S. and China in the South China Sea, which is not going to be developed into major conflicts soon, actually has little to do with the international law. It is more like a US strategic maneuver to defuse its competitor, and the international law happens to be one of its handy tools.

Conclusion

Despite the repeated explanation by Chinese government on its threefold intention in bringing up the OBOR initiative, which is aimed at: firstly, relieving the huge negative impacts of the stimulus package of RMB 4 trillion back in 2008; secondly, exploring overseas markets beyond Europe and North America; thirdly, counterbalancing the pressure against the backdrop of the US Pivot to Asia strategy. The OBOR initiative is not a calculation to attract confrontation with India or attaining strategic supremacy in the region, but India's suspicion and resistance to the MSR persists as usual. As one of the most needed partners of the MSR, India is alienating itself from China and its proposal for joint-exploration in South Asia on the economic, social and policy fronts, while both parties have become increasingly dependent upon each other in economic term. On one hand, it reveals the prevailing dichotomy in India's policy towards its immediate neighbor to the north. On the other hand, it indicates that China still lacks sufficient understanding of India's deep sense of insecurity.

Firstly, India's putting a very high stake in building up its relations with the only super power, because its national interests are best safeguarded in a multi-polar world. Despite its closer ties with the US under Bush and Obama administrations, Indian foreign policy based on strategic autonomy hasn't changed much. India can easily see through the US plot in accommodating to its core national interests, and remembers clearly how poor this partnership could become. The trust deficit between India and the US is notable due to the fundamental differences over issues ranging from trade to human rights. Secondly, India's influence over the states in its periphery is no longer that strong as the old days, and the political developments in the states such as Sri Lanka, Maldives and Nepal is gradually sliding out of its control. When the states in its backyard are looking beyond New Delhi for aid and assistance, Beijing always appears on their priority list. Considering the urgent need to maintain its growth at a proper speed, the Chinese Government and the enterprises can hardly deny the temptation. Thirdly, the American designed hypothesis of the String of Pearls strategy, focusing on China's military appetite in the Indian Ocean, has found its way into the nerve of Indian strategic community.

Chinese leadership has realized that it might be a mistake to put too much emphasis on a series of infrastructure projects along the maritime route from China's coastal area to Europe, while inadequate efforts was made to understand the concerns and the real need of states along the route. It is undeniable that India has developed an impression that China focuses its attention only on expanding its economic, political and military influence in a previously unfamiliar sphere, when China tries hard to enhance the convergence between the two through devising a mutually acceptable co-prosperity scheme. Somehow, India's defeat in the 1962 war has become a burden on China's shoulder. When China decided to make up for the opportunities lost to both parties, there usually came the opposite of the intended effects. As per my understanding, in the eyes of India, the OBOR initiative has started off on the wrong foot, and it will remain unacceptable as long as it implies a never-widening gap between China and India, unless a major modification on its South Asian episode as per India's requests, which is most possibly under Chinese leadership's serious consideration for the moment.

End Notes

1   In 2014, China's total goods trade with the ASEAN Region was USD 480 billion, China Beating US in Trade Volume with ASEAN Nations, 14 Aug 2015, http://sputniknews.com/us/20150814/1025732933.html accessed on

2   India has the largest population of youth in the world with about 66% of the population under the age of 35. In September 2015, the unemployment reached a mark that 23 lakh people applied for 368 posts of peon in the state secretariat in Uttar Pradesh. Among the applicants, 255 candidates with a PhD degree and more than two lakh hold BTech, BSc, Mcom and MSc degrees. Ramandeep Kaur, Unemployment on rise in India, http://www.mapsofindia.com/my-india/society/unemployment-on-rise-in-india

3   *"Total Trade, Country-wise Top n countries", Department of Commerce, Ministry of Commerce & Industry, Government of India, http://commerce.nic. in/eidb/default.asp*

4   The China India bilateral trade for financial year 2014-2015 was USD 758,371.89 million, *Department of Commerce, Export Import Data Bank,* http://commerce.nic.in/eidb/iecnt.asp accessed on

5   The purpose for tax evasion is the primary reason for the Indian importers to write off most of the business transaction with their Chinese partners when submitting tax forms to the Indian Government, Aman Agarwal of Indian Institute of Finance, Q&A sessions, International Symposium *"One Belt One Road: Vision and Roadmap for China India Cooperation"*, Sichuan University, China, 29-30 November 2015

6   Scott Kennedy, David A. Parker, Building China's "One Belt, One Road", Critical Questions, 3 Apr 2015, Center for Strategic and International Studies

7   China and the Making of an Alternative Order: Figuring Out the Indian Debate, Dr. Jagannath Panda, Research Fellow, IDSA, New Delhi, 1 April 2015, a lecture at Institute of China Studies, New Delhi.

8   The World Bank's ease of doing business survey, released in October, has ranked India at 130 out of 189 countries. http://www.doingbusiness.org/data/ exploreeconomies/india accessed on

9   Japan, India Sign $12B Bullet Train Deal, Agree On Peaceful Nuclear Energy Cooperation, 12 December 2015, http://www.ibtimes.com/japan-india-sign-12b-bullet-train-deal-agree-peaceful-nuclear-energy-cooperation-2222994 accessed on

10 TG Suresh, Jawaharlal Nehru University, *China's New Silk Road Initiative: A Transnational Development Model?* International Symposium *"One Belt One Road: Vision and Roadmap for China India Cooperation"*, Sichuan University, China, 29-30 November 2015

11 Raja Mohan, Chinese Takeaway: One Belt, One Road, August 13, 2014, http:// carnegieendowment.org/2014/08/13/chinese-takeaway-one-belt-one-road

12 中非双边贸易额2013年突破两千亿美元，22 April 2014，http://news.xinhua net.com/fortune/2014-04/22/c_1110359145.htm accessed on

Section II

One Belt One Road: India's Perspective

3

Continental Aspect of the 'One Belt One Road': India's Perspective

Nivedita Das Kundu

The 'One Belt One Road', (OBOR) is an omnibus word for a series of Transport Corridor initiatives made by China primarily, but not limited to China, but to the Eurasian, South Asian and South East Asian region too as well as, towards the Indian Ocean region, connecting East with the West trying to revive the ancient silk road connectivity. Like other Chinese projects in recent times, this is also a gigantic proposal initiated by China. The "One Belt One Road," (OBOR) initiative has enabled China to become the epicentre of regional as well as global economics and geopolitics. This initiative has two major elements the initiatives on 'Land' and initiatives at 'Sea' called the 'Silk Road Economic Belt' and the 'Maritime Silk Road', respectively. These transport connectivity and transport corridors aim to connect the nations increasing communication and network system. In today's international environment, commonality of the key national interest and good economic relations creates possibility for cooperation. The debate on China's 'One Belt One Road' in China is mainly to improve the linkages and increase the regional cooperation and develop trade and economic relations. Nonetheless, with the OBOR initiatives China is also seen using commerce as a tool to expand its geopolitical and geostrategic influence. This chapter tries to highlight various aspects on "One Belt One Road "giving India's perspective. The chapter would try to bring forth the insights, which helps in understanding the debates on new geo-political reality and trade and economic development through possible regional cooperation.

OBOR may be conceptualized as interplay of at least two competing discourses i.e. discourse of initiating new regionalism and discourse of increasing connectivity and economic cooperation reflecting different discursive practices. The argument given is that "One Belt One Road", has got the capacity to become modern transportation and communication road, increasing trade as well as people to people contact. The idea is to bring forth the insights, which helps in understanding the debate on potential regional cooperation. The questions that were essentially addressed while working on this chapter is on the present discourse on OBOR. Whether OBOR is only Economic or Strategic initiative? What are the geostrategic implication and challenges that need to be addressed? Can security concerns dampen the prospect for the OBOR projects? What factors are working in favour & what are the constrains while India-China working jointly on OBOR project?

OBOR: Concept

The OBOR initiative by China, incorporates a gamut of interactions be it transportation, culture, trade and economy. 'The Belt and Road' Initiative's, (BRI's) physical segments to the North is the 'land Route' that cuts across Eurasia and to the South there is the 'Maritime Silk Road', commencing in the Chinese Coast passing through South East Asia into Indian Ocean touching several ports en route before terminating in Europe. [1]

New regional Institutions, such as the 'Asian Infrastructure Investment Bank' (AIIB) and 'New Silk Road Fund' (NSRF), are designed in part to complement and support the 'Belt and Road development purpose.[2] There have been debates across the world regarding different facets of the 'Belt and Road' initiative. The view and vision expressed by the Chinese White Paper on the OBOR/BRI is that it is primarily economic in nature, even though there are parallel initiatives in culture, education, technology advancement, healthcare and other domains.[3] From the economic perspective, it is clear that OBOR/BRI is the next major step to spur the growth of Chinese economy. However, it is natural that such a vast and ambitious network invariably requires certain degree of security guarantees even though it has not been articulated in the ambitious OBOR vision document.

Land Road

The land corridors formulating under the OBOR/BRI initiative has ensured new regionalism and it is expected that this initiation will be a successful outcome of the deep neighbourhood integration policy and network diplomacy. New regionalism can be established by reviving connectivity through transport network.[4] However, proper access between or among the countries for economic integration and regional cooperation needs to be maintained. The Silk Road represents a phenomenon of the political and cultural integration. The conceptual as well as the practical challenge was to devise a framework to create channels and mechanisms for interaction and cooperation that would accelerate economic development and widen the sphere of connectivity.[5]

All the three basic components i.e. geographical proximity, technological feasibility and economic viability favours formation of new regionalism.[6] However, proper access between or among the countries for economic integration and regional cooperation needs to be maintained,[7] for bringing down the gaps while promoting regional integration.[8] Hence, it is expected that under OBOR the land corridor projects can help in the regional cooperation by improving the connectivity.

Transport Networks: Regional Integration

The 'One Belt One Road', is expected to improve the network of trade routes that for centuries criss-crossed the Asian-European continent and yielded immense commercial benefits and also fostered a lively cross-cultural fertilization. Today, the idea to revitalize the Silk Roads connectivity is also suggesting that all that is needed is to reconnect distant parts of the world merely to retrace old pathways increasing geo-strategic significance of this connectivity. Numbers of regional transport corridor projects have already started making the regional integration possible.

- Iran showed keenness to expand its railways, roads, ports, and telecom sector and energy security for regional development.

- Gwadar Port is being developed into the most accessible international trade routes to connect the Central Asian Republics and China's Xinjiang border region.

- TASIM (Trans-Eurasian Information Super Highway) transit line is expected to stretch through China, Kazakhstan, Azerbaijan, Georgia and Turkey to Germany bringing East closer to West.[9]

- TRACCECA[10]project connecting Armenia, Azerbaijan, Georgia, Kazakhstan, Kyrgyzstan, Tajikistan, Turkmenistan, Uzbekistan, Mongolia, Ukraine, Moldavia, Turkey, Bulgaria, Romania, and Iran is another significant connectivity project enabling to bring Asian as well as countries from Caucasus closer to each other.

- TUTAP is the regional electricity connectivity project, this is connecting Turkmenistan, Uzbekistan, and Tajikistan and expected to connect Afghanistan and possibly to India and Pakistan too.

- The southern corridor of the Trans-Asian Railway is one of four corridor studies undertaken as part of the Asian Land Transport Infrastructure Development (ALTID) project. The principal function of this corridor is to allow railway transport containers to move between South Asia and Europe, Southern China and Europe and Thailand and Europe. The Southern Corridor is also expected to go from Europe to Southeast Asia, connecting Turkey, Iran, Pakistan, India, Bangladesh, Myanmar, and Thailand, with links to China's Yunnan Province via Malaysia to Singapore.[11]

- The Trans-Asian Railway (TAR) is a project to create an integrated freight railway network across Europe and Asia. [12]

OBOR: India Connect

Many roads of the 'Belt' under OBOR initiative are inching towards India. Throughout the history of Silk Road many scholars and businessmen from India visited China and vice - versa. Beijing is urging New Delhi to jointly develop a trans-Himalayan economic zone of cooperation with Nepal and Bhutan. Beijing has also been talking to New Delhi about the BCIM (Bangladesh, China, India and Myanmar) corridor to link the Yunnan province in south-western China with Myanmar, Bangladesh and with eastern India. It is no secret that India till date did not show much enthusiasm in joining the OBOR initiatives but India definitely taking a fresh look on this issue. Today India is also upgrading its connectivity, modernising border management, building new ports and developing better coordination between the government and corporate entities on taking up these projects.[13] India is willing to cooperate with China on increasing regional connectivity, as India does not want marginalisation from the unfolding geo-economic transformation in Asia and in the Indo-Pacific region, however, cerain concerns needs to be addressed jointly

Since May 2013, BCIM route is reportedly discussed between the Indian and Chinese leaders regularly. The BCIM route is expected to connect Kunming to Kolkata, linking Mandalay in Myanmar further connecting Dhaka and Chittagong. Pursuant to the understanding reached between the two countries in May 2013, India and China have established a Study Group on the BCIM Economic Corridor.[14] With joint efforts by China, India, Myanmar and Bangladesh, this route is expected to become important trade connectivity, however, security issues need to be addressed simultaneously and talks are in process for addressing sensitive security concerns in the region.

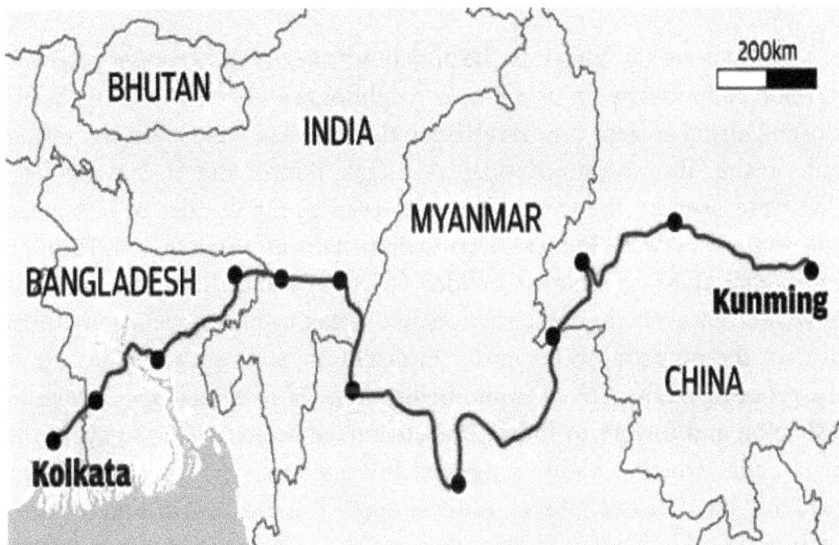

Fig. 3.1 BCIM Map

Source:https://www.google.co.in/search?q=Map+of+BCIM&biw=1366&bih=667 &source=lnms&tbm=isch&sa=X&ved=0ahUKEwjFkumnuXLAhULU44KHRqI CE0Q_AUIBygC#imgrc=uenln9sOUyXVX

India would be interested in exploring the opportunities coming through OBOR. However, India's interest would be mainly to support the project to get the economic benefit, but security matters needs to be addressed jointly for enhancing the regional cooperation. The regional cooperation could be beneficial for tracking regional terrorism and developing capabilities to respond to future uncertainties. [15] The idea of connecting with OBOR might serve as an advantageous for India, helping to open-up a new path for formulating India's long-term domestic as well as foreign policy strategy.

India is ideally positioned today to expand the volume and direction of trade. Through regional transport initiatives, India could initiate the route revitalization process in view of globalization and economic integration. India has already started renewing the age-old relations with its extended neighbours in Eurasia for reviving Silk Road connectivity. This is essential for the development of the region, however, some potential branches are yet to be revived to realize the regional cooperation and for the overall development.

India is also looking into the possibility of extending cooperation and develop connectivity for bringing its neighbours and extended neighbours closer. During ancient time Azerbaijan the Eurasian State was a significant hub on the Silk ways. Even today, Ateshgah Temple and *Saraies* (Motels) that were used by the traders are preserved as a reminder of Silk Road connectivity between India and Azerbaijan in the Eurasian region. Through International North South Corridor (INSTC) route this connectivity is now revived, also the construction of Ashkelon-Eilat pipeline to India has got the potential to bring few Eurasian States closer to India and in the process Azerbaijan's oil could be brought via tankers from Ceyhan to Ashkelon and further to India[16] The advantage here could be to avoid the Suez Canal, which is highly congested and not accessible to super tankers, reducing the time taken for oil tankers to reach India from around 40 days to 19 days and this would also open up the vast energy reserves of the Caspian Sea to India.

Turkmenistan-Afghanistan-Pakistan-India (TAPI) gas pipeline project is another significant connectivity project under the revival of Silk Road connectivity initiative, the construction of TAPI has already started. This is an important connectivity project to meet the growing energy needs of South Asian States. TAPI proposes to deliver gas from Dovletabad gas fields of Turkmenistan to Pakistan and India via Afghanistan. TAPI gas pipeline project has been described as modern days 'Pipeline for Peace' and a 'Reflection of Desire'. The implementation of TAPI project has enabled to bring Central Asia and South Asia much closer. This projects has got the potential to integrate regional countries for development and prosperity.[17]TAPI can support by providing natural gas for fulfilling the economic development plans and for implementing clean energy program on the regional countries. TAPI is expected to become a best example of growing regional integration process under the Silk Road connectivity projects.

International North-South Transport Corridor (INSTC) is significant regional transport corridor project initiated by India, Iran and Russia. This is extremely promising project and trying to revive the Silk Road connectivity linking east with the west and the regional countries by rail, ship and by road ways for moving freight from South Asia through Central Asia, South Caucasus and Russia to Europe. India signed an agreement mainly with Russia and Iran in 2001 to develop this road. The road primarily involves moving goods from India via ship to Iran, from Iran; the freight could be moved by ship across the Caspian Sea or by truck or rail to Southern Russia, and goods are transported by truck or rail along the Volga River through Moscow to the Northern Europe.[18] India has taken a major step by coordinating with the countries like Iran, Russia and the countries of Central Asia, as well as Bulgaria, to push the idea of this project and for its implementation.

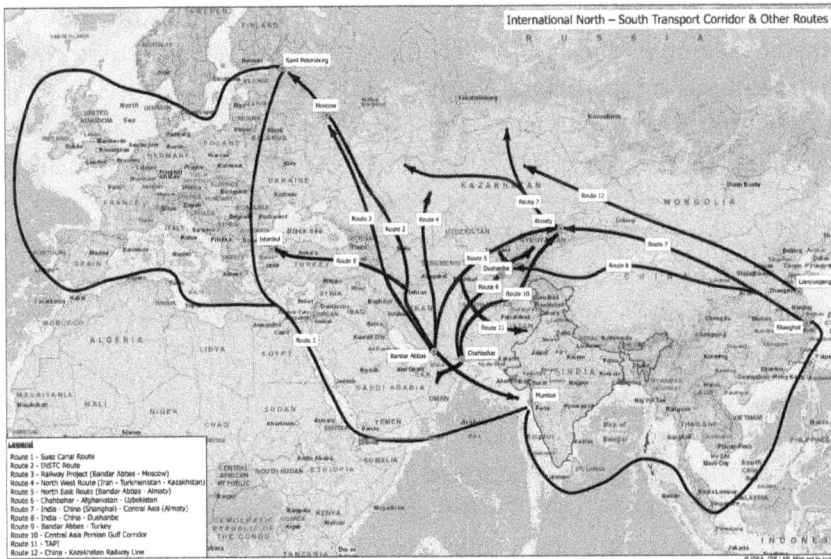

Fig. 3.2 Map of International North South Corridor and other Routes

Source: http://www.idsa.in/issuebrief/International NorthSouth Transport Corridor_msroy_180815

Currently, INSTC project includes regional countries such as Azerbaijan, Armenia, Kazakhstan, Kyrgyzstan, Tajikistan, Turkmenistan, Turkey, Syria, Ukraine, Belarus and also Oman. India emphasized on the need to increase cooperation and connectivity between the regional countries for mutual benefit. North-south corridor intends to facilitate this prospect and bring the powers of the region together. This project envisages a multi-modal transportation network that connects ports on India's west coast to Bandar Abbas in Iran, then overland to Bandar Anzali port on the Caspian Sea. Further, through Rasht and Astara moves further towards Russia and through Mediterranean to the Ukrainian ports of Odessa and Kiev and then onwards to Russia.[19]

The INSTC route also has the rail connectivity of about 200 km from Iran to the Caspian Sea region. There is a possibility that in near future this network can be further expanded towards the South East Asia. While the Suez Canal route takes about 45-60 days, this Green Corridor project (INSTC) through Iran will significantly reduce transportation time and cost. It is expected that the INSTC route will take about 25-30 days reducing the transportation time significantly. INSTC will also reduce the transportation costs and eliminate the problems related to the legal issues such as vehicle weights, dimensions and operating permits, inconsistent documentation and inspections etc. INSTC is expected to move through Nhava Sheva port in Mumbai (India) Bandar Abbas (Iran)-Tehran-Bandar Anzali (Iran)-Astrakhan (Russia). India is now keenly looking into the fast construction of Gazvin-Rasht-Astara (Iran)-Astara (Azerbaijan) railway route for connecting the railway lines of INSTC connectivity.[20] It is expected that both the trade and tourism prospect will increase through this transport corridor. India welcomes China's participation in INSTC and expand the OBOR connectivity connecting East with the West, through INSTC linkages.

OBOR: Debates and Discourse

In India there are various opinion and views that are shared on the OBOR. Some consider China's OBOR initiative as a significant regional project where as some are not much enthusiastic about this. Discourse on OBOR among policy makers, analysts and practitioners in India are such that if the dispute over the South China Sea is not resolved or eased, it will not be conducive to the success of 'One Belt One Road'. Some feels 'One Belt One Road' initiative can better integrate ASEAN countries. But some argue that not every country in the region will reap equal benefits. Some argue that Western Nations will oppose OBOR's move as they have fear that China might try to challenge the western international political and economic order through OBOR projects. Others mention that investing in infrastructure projects along the "One Belt One Road", could be beneficial whereas, some are of the opinion that it is likely to give China a bigger say in global economic and political affairs.

Some scholars views that if China does not skilfully balance investments and diplomacy it may find itself tangled in conflicts for which it is not prepared. Some political analysts mentioned that developing nations would be given a prominent role in the governance of the Beijing-led Asian Infrastructure Investment Bank (AIIB) and rebuke existing international financing institutions for failing to serve their needs. Some argue that China-sponsored AIIB will present a new narrative on international development financing – just as IMF and World Bank. Some believe AIIB will promote alternate principles. Many analysts believe that OBOR route that might run through some of China's poorest and least developed region could provide stimulus to help, cushion the effects of the deep economic slowdown in China. Some are of the opinion that there will be a need to have an environment protection projects for enabling large-scale, transnational investment in Asia.

Some are of the view that OBOR would strengthen China's importance as an economic partner for its neighbours and potentially enhance Beijing's diplomatic leverage in the region. Some are also of the opinion that increased investment in energy and mineral resources, particularly in Central Asia and Russia could also help reduce China's reliance on commodities imported from overseas, including oil transiting the Strait of Malacca; hence China would encourage this move through OBOR initiative

Few India's policy makers are also of the opinion that China's investments in India's immediate neighbourhood through OBOR initiative like in Sri Lanka, Nepal, Pakistan, and Bangladesh might heighten geopolitical tensions.

Views expressed by India's Foreign Minister Sushma Swaraj on June 2015, calling the OBOR's China-Pakistan Economic Corridor (CPEC) project 'unacceptable' since it crosses through Indian Territory.

Views expressed by India's Foreign Secretory Dr. S. Jaishankar at Fullerton Lecture on 22 July 2015, is that 'China's 'One Belt One Road' initiative need to link China to countries, cities and ports across the Eurasian landmass. China would need to obtain broader approval for the projects from other countries in the region for moving forward and where India stand is that, if this is something in which China want a larger participation, then there would be a need for a large discussion but that hasn't happened yet.'

However, India's former Foreign Secretary Shyam Saran mentioned during his lecture at ICS (Institute of Chinese Studies), New Delhi, on October 9th 2015, "Currently, India has neither the resources nor the economic weight to put in place competitive and alternative connectivity networks on a global scale, therefore, now it may be worthwhile to carefully evaluate those components of the OBOR which may, in fact, improve India's own connectivity to major markets and resource supplies and become participants in them just as India chose to do with the AIIB & NDB (New Development Bank)".

While Dr. Jaishanker delivering a keynote address on "Asia: Regional and Global Connectivity" at the Raisina Dialogue in New Delhi, on 2nd March, 2016, mentioned that, "New Delhi viewed the grand connectivity initiative by Chinese President Xi Jinping distinctly from the Asian Infrastructure Investment Bank (AIIB), which was also conceived by Beijing, but was set up by over 50 nations collectively, hence, as the interactive dynamic between strategic interests and connectivity initiatives is an universal proposition and is on particular display in our continent, the key issue is whether we will build our connectivity through consultative processes or through more unilateral decisions." Foreign secretary added that "India's preference is for the former." As per Dr. Jaishankar, "Connectivity should diffuse national rivalries, not add to regional tensions".

OBOR: Concerns and Differences

Given the opaque nature of the OBOR, it doesn't pose an open threat to India's national security. But unravelling the details of the OBOR suggests subtle security concerns and challenges for India.[21] India has shown concern over OBOR's China-Pakistan Economic Corridor (CPEC) project. As per India CPEC Project under the OBOR initiative might yield far-reaching economic benefits but can have serious security implications too. India and

China differ in opinion on CPEC. As per India, the Karakoram (land) with Gwadar (sea) alignment has both commercial and military significance to serve as a strategic choke-points vis-à-vis India.

India's concern is such that CPEC might also prevent Af-Pak region from potentially becoming a safer place once US troops leaves Afghanistan.[22] Moreover, reports suggests that Pakistan is now working on raising the constitutional status of Gilgit-Baltistan (G-B) region in a bid to provide legal cover to the ambitious China-Pakistan Economic Corridor (CPEC). The Pakistan's move could signal a historic shift in country's position on the future of the wider Kashmir region[23]. Looking into the PoK's (Pakistan occupied Kashmir's) location and Pakistan's stand on GB (Gilgit-Baltistan) India showed concern over CPEC,[24] as per India CPEC could bring serious ramification for India in addressing security concerns which needs cautious approach.

Fig. 3.3 Map of CPEC

Source:http://www.idsa.in/policybrief/ATaleofTwoDisputesChinasIrrationality andIndiasStakes_rdahiya_290615

However, as per China the CPEC is considered as a 'livelihood project', under the OBOR initiative, not being 'political' and are just 'commercial' in nature. As per China, the CPEC project is designed to connect Kashgar in China's Xinjiang Province with the strategic port of Gwadar in Pakistan.[25] Whear-as, India feels CPEC, runs through a territory that is historically Indian Territory, hence, considers this as a disputed part. India has always maintained that Gilgit-Baltistan is part of the princely state of Jammu and Kashmir (J&K), which had acceded to India.[26] Therefore, India's concern over China-Pakistan understanding on the Gwadar Port is noteworthy.[27] Even though China has maintained a somewhat 'neutral' position on the Kashmir issue in recent years particularly since the 'Kargil war', terming this as a 'bilateral historical dispute'. However, the Chinese pursuit of the CPEC project may impel China to revisit its position on Kashmir in future.[28] CPEC is expected to be connected with the Gwadar port in four key areas, namely, port, energy, infrastructure and industrial cooperation. *While* China defends CPEC, calling it a 'commercial' or 'livelihood' project, as per India, then the 'commercial' activity carried out by India for oil and energy exploration in the SCS (South China Sea) should not come under doubt.[29] India is concerned as there is no explanation, for China's $46 billion dollar investment made in Pakistan, the country which is experiencing political instability and armed violence.[30] The CPEC is estimated to involve an initial $46 billion investment in infrastructure development programme. Reports indicate that China will now run the Karot Hydropower project, which is roughly estimated to cost $1.65 billion, for the next 30 years before handing it over to Pakistan. The CPEC project is likely to be operationalized by 2020.[31]

India also expressed concern over proposed trilateral economic corridor involving China-Nepal-India (CNI). Understandably, India's response has been lukewarm, as there is an apprehension that the trade balance between India and Nepal might slowdown in favour of China. The argument given is such that a direct economic corridor between India and China requires the Line of Actual Control (LAC) to be delineated at least in some sectors. Such delineation will enable the creation of customs centres and other paraphernalia required for cross-border trade. India is concerned that as it appears China does not foresee the possibility of delineating the Line of Actual Control (LAC) in the coming years even in some sectors for establishing direct economic corridor between India and China. As per India's policy makers China is exploring the possibilities of accessing Indian market through third countries that is through CPEC, the BCIM and the CNI without even delineating the LAC, that is the concern coming up under the OBOR discourse in India .[32]

OBOR: Challenges

Any radical policy could increase the risk of chaos for OBOR's success and could even decrease the scope of OBOR's prospect. There is a challenge in number of sectors for smooth flow of trade and economic connectivity:

(i)   Challenge in handling the customs issues for easy trade and economic cooperation.

(ii) Challenge in smooth and quick visa processing activities.

(iii) There is a complication in simplifying the Banking procedures for conducting smooth commercial activities.

(iv) Lack of information poses another major challenge in communicating correct information.

OBOR: Recommendations

To overcome the challenges:

(i)   There is a need to conduct regular dialogue & interaction; i.e. the Consultative approach needs to be applied.

(ii) There is a need to discuss about the cooperation mechanism possibilities at regular interval with the concerned authorities of all the partner countries.

(iii) There is also a need to implement collective security programme initiative.

(iv) There is a need for greater transparency for alignment of roads and for sharing of information at the same time the vision should be clear and unified.

(v)   There is a need for better coordination and harmonize the strategies complimenting each other's requirement.

(vi) There should be clarity for the Institutional regulatory systems. For the legal, digital as well as for the financial aspects. At the same time, all the stake holders should be consulted for the formulation process.

(vii) OBOR initiative can follow the approach that other multilateral organistions like ASEAN, (Association for the South-East Asian Nations), SAARC, (South Asian Association for Regional Cooperation) ReCAAP (regional cooperation agreement on combatting piracy and armed robbery against ships in Asia) are following.

(viii) There is a need to work for building strategic trust between the partner countries.

Conclusion

There is a competitive advantage in China's OBOR initiative; the OBOR projects could realize the advantage of the regional countries. It is also important to note that in today's world, strategic and economic cooperation go hand in hand, hence, there is a need to formulate an intense economic and trade relationship for maintaining cooperation with each other. If successfully carried out, then OBOR initiative could make the entire region covered with a great infrastructure of highways, railways and logistics Centers as well as commercial hubs and these initiatives could take care of fast movement of both passengers and cargoes. China through OBOR initiative has put forward its ambition and imaginations, however, should also consider regional security issues and concerns seriously while working on OBOR projects and transparency needs to be maintained at the same time the trust factor has to be increased. To conclude, must mention that there will be several obstacles and challenges but there will be a need to look into new diplomatic, economic and security realities on the ground to acquire the benefits and the expectations through OBOR projects and make this as a successful regional initiative.

End Notes

1   Report of National Development and Reform Commission, Ministry of Foreign Affairs, and Ministry of Commerce of the People's Republic of China, with State Council authorization, March 2015, Beijing, available at http:// news.xinhuanet.com/english/china/2015-03/28/c_134105858.htm , accessed on November 5, 2015.

2   During the last two years, China has built 15 airports and expanded another 28 in provinces along the routes of the OBOR. China is now working on increasing direct aerial connectivity with Eurasian states to increase the linkages under OBOR mission. Over the last few years in the satellite technology arena, China has made phenomenal progress, various real-time inputs provided by their multiple satellite constellations are also expected to support significantly in conducting various traffic planning and management activities on land and sea routes under OBOR initiative

3   'Space Silk Road' to help aviation, shipping, disaster relief, http://www. wantchinatimes.com/news-subclass-cnt.aspx?id=20150603000007&c id=1101, accessed on October 17, 2015

4   Hussain Moazzen, Lyanlur Islam, Reza kibra, *South Asian Economic development: transformation opportunities and challenges*, Routledge, London, New York, 1999

5   AkinerShirin, IbrahimovRovshan, ArizHuseynov, 'Interregional cooperation in Eurasia: Transport and Logistic projects as an accelerator of Integration within and between the Black sea region, the South Caucasus and Central Asia', Special double issue, Vol.9-10, September 2013,pp 113-116

6   HussainMoazzen,Lyanlur Islam, Reza kibra, *South Asian Economic development: transformation opportunities and challenges*, Routledge, London, New York, 1999

7   Information shared by the Turkish diplomat on 7th July2014

8   AkinerShirin, IbrahimovRovshan, ArizHuseynov, 'Interregional cooperation in Eurasia: Transport and Logistic projects as an accelerator of Integration within and between the Black sea region, the South Caucasus and Central Asia', Special double issue, Vol.9-10, September 2013,pp 113-116.

9   Kundu Das Nivedita, Yulak Murat, Humbatov Mahir in "Baku-Tiblisi-Kars Railroads:The Iron ground for the Silk Road"," Sam Review", Volume 13, September 2014, pp.28, 30 & 42

10 Ibid

11 Ibid

12 This project was initiated in the 1960s, with the objective of providing a continuous 8,750 miles (14,080 km) rail link between South East Asia with South Asia and with possible further connections to Europe and Africa. By

the 1990s, the end of the Cold War and normalisation of relations improved the prospects for creating a rail network across the Asian continent.

13 Vaid Manish and Singh Maini Tridivesh, "BCIM: Can India Be a Driving Force?" *The Diplomat* available at http://thediplomat.com/2015/01/bcim-can-india-be-a-driving-force/accessed on15 , June, 2015

14 Stobdan P. "Carving out a path on Chinas road", available at http://www.thehindu.com/opinion/columns/world-view-column-carving-out-a-path-on-chinas-road/article7814833.ece

15 Sahoo Pravakar and Bhunia Abhirup, "BCIM Corridor a Game Changer for South Asian Trade", *East Asia Forum*, available at http://www.eastasiaforum.org/2014/07/18/bcim-corridor-a-game-changer-for-south-asian-trade/ accessed on November 7, 2015

16 The oil could fed into the Ashkelon–Eilat pipeline, which could bring it to Eilat on the Gulf of Aqaba, from there, Eilat tankers could bring Azerbaijan's oil to Mumbai.Kundu Das Nivedita, "Prospects for India-Azerbaijan Energy Cooperation", *CCEE Policy Brief*, Caspian Center for Energy and Environment, ADA University, Azerbaijan, June, 2014. also available at *file:///C:/Users/rinku%20kundu/Downloads/CCEE%20Policy%20Brief-6%20(5).pdf*

17 Kundu Das Nivedita, "Turkmenistan-Afghanistan-Pakistan-India (TAPI) Pipeline Project from Dream to reality", available at valdai club.com/TAP Pipeline Project from Dream to reality/ December 16, 2015

18 Kundu Das Nivedita, Murat Yulek & Humbatov Mahir, "Baku-Tbilisi-Kars Railroads : The Iron Ground For The Silk Road", Sam Review, Volume 13, September 2014, Center for Strategic Studies, Baku, Azerbaijan, pp.31-34

19 Ibid

20 Ibid

21 Panda Jagganath, Does China's 'One Belt, One Road' initiative poses any threat to India's national security?   http://www.idsa.in/askanexpert/Q1887Does Chinas One Belt One Road accessed on 16 June, 2015

22 Sibbal Kawal Speech in December 9, 2015, on "China's Growing Influence in India's Neighbourhood and Implications for India", USI, New Delhi, attended by author.

23 Kumar Sanjay, "Merger of Gilgit-Baltistan into Pakistan – Ramifications", available at usiblog.in/author/sanjaykumar/ accessed on January 26,2015 Recently, proposal mentioned for the first time in Pakistan's constitution for bringing this mountainous region a step closer to being fully absorbed as an additional province. Moreover, Islamabad has historically insisted that the part of Kashmir it controls are semi-autonomous and has not formally integrated them into the country, in line with its position that a referendum should be carried out from across whole of the region

24   The G-B area of Jammu and Kashmir occupied by Pakistan covers 85,793 sq km. It was further divided in 1970 into two separate administrative divisions, Mirpur-Muzaffarabad (which Pakistan calls Azad Jammu and Kashmir, or AJK) and the Federally Administered Gilgit-Baltistan. G-B was earlier referred to as the "Northern Areas" in Pakistan. Both the regions have their own legislative assemblies and, technically, are not part of the Pakistan federation. Pakistan administers them through a special minister for Kashmir and joint councils. Pakistan maintained that Kashmir is a disputed region and that its status should be decided by a plebiscite under the UN resolution of 1948-49. Reportedly, the government of Pakistan-occupied Kashmir (PoK) has decided to lodge protest against any attempt to convert G-B into a province of Pakistan. Pakistan-occupied Kashmir (PoK) Prime Minister Chaudhry Abdul Majeed has warned Islamabad against any attempt to convert G-B into a federal province. PoK President Sardar Mohammad Yaqoob Khan warned that such a step would be more damaging than the dismemberment of Pakistan in 1971.The ministers are of the view that making G-B a province of Pakistan will dent the Kashmir cause. They maintain that G-B is part and parcel of the state of Jammu and Kashmir and any attempt to merge it into Pakistan will deal a fatal blow to their stance in the light of the UN resolution. They maintain that Pakistan has been given administrative control of G-B on a temporary basis only and Pakistan must not attempt to change its identity

25   Opinion shared by Professor Yang-minghong during the   Conference attended by author on "One Belt One Road: Vision and Road Map of China India cooperation", Sichuan University, Chengdu, China on 28th November 2015, attended by author

26   Opinion shared by Bring. Vinod Ananad during a Conference attended by author on "One Belt One Road", Sichuan University, Chengdu, China on 28th November 2015, attended by author

27   Opinion expressed by Indian scholars during Round Table Discussion between Chinese and Indian scholars on "One Belt One Road", on August 9, 2015 at USI, New Delhi, attended by author

28   Kumar Sanjay, "Merger of Gilgit-Baltistan into Pakistan – Ramifications", avilable at http://usiblog.in/?s=CPEC+by+Sanjay, accessed on March 16th 2016

29   Opinion Shared by Gen. Singh and Gen. Sandhu during the talk and discussion between Chinese and Indian scholars on "China Pakistan economic Corridor", on January 20, 2016 at USI, New Delhi, attended by author.

30   Shyam Saran "What China's One Belt and One Road Strategy Means for India, Asia and the World", avialble at http://thewire.in/2015/10/09/what-chinas-one-belt-and-one-road-strategy-means-for-india-asia-and-the-world-12532/ accessed on November 2, 2015

31 Pulipake Sanjay India must capitalise on transnational economic corridors "The Financial, Express", February 13, 2016, available at http://www. financialexpress.com/article/fe-columnist/india-must-capitalise-on-transnational-economic-corridors/211024/ accessed on 3rd March 2016

32 Ibid.

References

Alan Lee Boyer, Recreating the Silk Road: The Challenges of over-coming transaction costs, China and Eurasia Vol. IV, No.4, Central Asia- Caucasus Institute and Silk Route Studies Programme, 2006, pp.72-74.

Richard Foltz, Religions of the Silk Road, Palgrave Macmillan, New York, 2nd edition, 2010

C.M. Hogan, Burnham A. ed. Silk Road, North China, the Megalithic Portal and Megalith Map, http://www.megalithic.co.uk/article.php?sid=18006. 13th July, 2011

Boulnois Luce, Silk Road: Monks, Warriors & Merchants, Odyssey Books, Hong Kong, 2005, p. 66.

Jaspers K, Sense and Perpouse of History, Moscow, 1994, p.141.

The Silk Roads: Highways of Culture and Commerce, UNESCO Publication, Berghahn Book, 2001

Ash Narain Roy, A Corridor of Prosperity, available at www.hardnewsmedia.com

G.M. Mir, "Resource management, regional cooperation and sustainable development states", New Delhi, 2003

Asia-Pacific | Asia takes first step on modern 'Silk Route'. BBC News. 05.01. 2013.

Eliseeff, "Approaches Old and New to the Silk Roads" in The Silk Roads: Highways of Culture and Commerce, Paris, 1998, UNESCO, Reprinted Berghahn Books,2009, pp. 1–2.

David Gosset, "Xinjiang and the revival of Silk Route", Greater China, 2000

Hussain Moazzen, Lyan lur Islam, Reza kibra, South Asian Economic development: transformation opportunities and challenges, Routledge, London, New York, 1999

World Bank Report, From Disintegration to Reintegration: Europe and Central Asia in International Trade,2006, available at http://www.worldbank.org/

S.Polanchek, Conflict and Trade, Journal of Conflict Resolution, Vol. 24 (1)1980, pp.55-78

Wilfred J.Ethier, Regionalism in a multilateral World, Journal of Political Economy, Vol.106 (6) December, 1998, pp.1214-12145

Silk Road, http://www.livius.org/sh-si/silk_road/silk_road.html, LIVIUS Articles of Ancient History, 28 October 2010

Seehttp://ec.europa.eu/europeaid/where/asia/regional-cooperation-central asia/transport/traceca_en.htm

World Bank Report, From Disintegration to re-integration: Europe and Central Asia in International Trade,2006, available at http://www.worldbank.Org

Ulric Killion, A Modern Chinese Journey to the West: Economic Globalization and Dualism, Nova Science Publishers, 2006, p.66

United Nation development Programme (UNDP), Human Development Report, 2994: Cultural library in today's diverse world," UNDP, New York 2004. Also see http://www.unescap.org/ttdw/index.asp?menuname=asianhighway

Waugh, Daniel. (2007), "Richthofen's "Silk Roads: Toward the Archaeology of a Concept." The Silk Road. Volume 5, Number 1, Summer 2007, p. 4

World Bank: trade and transport facilitation in Central Asia: Reducing the economic distance to markets", Final draft Report, 2005

"North South Corridor", Times of India Report, 13 March 2012

United Nations Economic and Social Commissions for Asia and the Pacific, "Transit Transport Issue in Landlocked and transit Developing Countries", Report No.ST/ESCAP/2270, 2003

Jean Francois Arvis, "Transit and the Special Case of landlocked Countries, Customs Mordernization Hand Book, Luc De Wulf and Jose B.Sokol, the World bank, Washington, DC, 2005

Prevas John, Envy of the Gods: Alexander the Great's Ill-Fated Journey across Asia, De Capo Press, Cambridge,2004, p121

Jerry H. Bentley,Old World Encounters: Cross-Cultural Contacts and Exchanges in Pre-Modern Times,New York: Oxford University Press, 1993,p. 32, 38-37,43-48

Dybo A.V., Chronology of Türkic languages and linguistic contacts of early Türks, Moscow, 2007, p. 786

Wink André, Al-Hind: The Making of the Indo-Islamic World, Brill Academic Publishers, 2002

Hays J.N., Epidemics and pandemics: their impacts on human history,2005, p.61

Arbrey, Patricia Buckley; Anne Walthall and James B. Palais, East Asia: A Cultural, Social, and Political History, Houghton Mifflin, 2nd revised edition 2008, p. 257

Yang Bin, Between Winds and Clouds: The Making of Yunnan. New York: Columbia University Press,2008

Foltz Richard C., Religions of the Silk Road: Overland Trade and Cultural Exchange from Antiquity to the Fifteenth Century. New York: St Martin's Press, 1999, pp. 37-47

Michel Sims, Harmonization and simplification of transport agreements, cross-border documents and transport regulations, Report Prepared for the Asian development bank, Manila 2005

Ian Jenkins and Paul Pezant, Central Asia: Reassessment of the Regional Transport Sector Strategy, A Report prepared for the Asian Development Bank, Manila, 2003. Also see http://www.orsam.org.tr/en/enUploads/Article/Files/201324_146%20ing.pdf

Boulnois, Luce (2005). Silk Road: Monks, Warriors & Merchants. Hong Kong: Odyssey Books. p. 66

See http://www.silkroadstudies.org/new/inside/publications/0505Conference_Total.pdf

Seehttp://www.realinstitutoelcano.org/wps/portal/rielcano_eng/Content?WCM_GLOBAL_CONTEXT=/elcano/elcano_in/zonas_in/dt59-2009

Central Eurasian Studies Review, available at http://www.cesr-cess.org/CESR_contribution.html accessed on 16th February 2011

Sikri Rajeev, Challenge & Strategy, Sage, India, 2009

Gael Raballand, Esen Ferhat, 'Economics and Politics of Cross border Oil Pipelines', Asia Europe Journal, Vol.5, (1), March 2007,pp.133-146

BP's Statistical Review of World Energy 2008

International Energy Outlook 2009, DOE/EIA

Stulberg Adam , 'Moving Beyond the Great Game', Geopolitics, Vol.10 (1), 2005,pp1-25.Svante E. Cornell, "Security Threats and Challenges in Caucasus after 9/11", in Ariel Cohen ed, Eursaia in Balance: The US and the Regional Power Shift, Aldershot: Ashgae Publishing Ltd, 2005, pp.44

Nakamur Yasushi, *Extractive Industries and 'Dutch Disease'*, Discussion Paper, 99/5, Department of Economics, Heriot-Watt University, 1999. Elisseeff, Vadime (2001). *The Silk Roads: Highways of Culture and Commerce.* UNESCO Publishing / Berghahn Books

Boulnois, Luce (2005). *Silk Road: Monks, Warriors & Merchants.* Hong Kong: Odyssey Books. p. 66

"Approaches Old and New to the Silk Roads" Eliseeff in: *The Silk Roads: Highways of Culture and Commerce.* Paris (1998) UNESCO, Reprint: Berghahn Books (2009), pp. 1–2

Waugh, Daniel. (2007), "Richthofen's "Silk Roads: Toward the Archaeology of a Concept." *The Silk Road.* Volume 5, Number 1, Summer 2007, p. 4

Prevas, John. (2004). *Envy of the Gods: Alexander the Great's Ill-Fated Journey across Asia*, p. 121. De Capo Press, Cambridge

The Megalithic Portal and Megalith Map. "Silk Road, North China", C.M. Hogan, the Megalithic Portal, ed. A. Burnham". Megalithic.co.uk. http://www. megalithic.co.uk/article.php?sid=18006. 13.07.2011

Jerry H. Bentley, *Old World Encounters: Cross-Cultural Contacts and Exchanges in Pre-Modern Times* (New York: Oxford University Press, 1993),p. 32

"Silk Road." http://www.livius.org/sh-si/silk_road/silk_road.html, LIVIUS Articles of Ancient History. 28 October 2010

Dybo A.V., *"Chronology of Türkic languages and linguistic contacts of early Türks"*,

Moskow, 2007, p. 786

Wink, André. Al-Hind: The Making of the Indo-Islamic World. Brill Academic Publishers, 2002

J. N. Hays (2005). *"Epidemics and pandemics: their impacts on human history"*. p.61

Arbrey, Patricia Buckley; Anne Walthall and James B. Palais (2nd rev ed 2008). *East Asia: A Cultural, Social, and Political History*, Houghton Mifflin. p. 257

"Asia-Pacific | Asia takes first step on modern 'Silk Route'. BBC News. 05.01. 2013

Ulric Killion, *A Modern Chinese Journey to the West: Economic Globalization And Dualism*, (Nova Science Publishers: 2006), p.66

Yang, Bin. (2008). *Between Winds and Clouds: The Making of Yunnan*. New York: Columbia University Press

Richard Foltz, *Religions of the Silk Road*, New York: Palgrave Macmillan, 2nd edition, 2010

Foltz, Richard C. (1999). *Religions of the Silk Road: Overland Trade and Cultural Exchange from Antiquity to the Fifteenth Century*. New York: St Martin's Press. pp. 37-47

Jerry H. Bentley, *Old World Encounters: Cross-Cultural Contacts and Exchanges in Pre-Modern Times* (New York: Oxford University Press, 1993), 43-48.

WTO Data Base of 7th November 2012

Michel Sims, "Harmonization and simplification of transport agreements, cross-Border Documents and Transport Regulations", Report Prepared for the Asian development bank, Manila 2005

Also see report issued by the National Development and Reform Commission, Ministry of Foreign Affairs, and Ministry of Commerce of the People's Republic of China, with State Council authorization, March 2015, Beijing, available at http://news.xinhuanet.com/english/china/2015-03/28/c_134105858.htm See, "China defends projects in POK, opposes India's oil exploration in South China Sea,"*Indian Express*, 4 June 2015, K.J.M. Varma, "China defends projects in Gilgit-Baltistan region, justifies its objections in SCS," *Live Mint*, 4 June 2015. One prominent China analyst in RTD held at USI mentioned that though a direct public statement has not been made by Chinese officials that China's current activities and investment in POK under the CPEC are based on the 1963 Agreement, Chinese officials and scholars often refer in their discussion to the 1963 agreement as one of the benchmarks of Chinese involvement and construction in POK. Besides, t Pakistani side always refers openly to the 1963 Agreement as the basis of China's involvement in POK.

"Q. NO. 260: Projects of China and Pakistan in Neighboring Countries", *Lok Sabha,* Starred Question No. 260 Answered On 10 December 2014, Ministry of External Affairs: Government of India

Also see Li Mingjian, "Chinese Debates of South China Sea Policy: Implications for Future Developments," *RSIS Working Paper,* No. 239, 17 May 2012

Chinese reports indicate that the 'nine-dash line' covers almost 80 per cent of the SCS on Chinese maps. In the Chinese estimation, the entire SCS zone is a total of 3.5 million sq km. China states that this 'nine-dash line' boundary was first published in an official map in 1948. Since then, China has officially based its claim on this map, and all the official maps released subsequently by the Chinese government carry this 'nine-dash line'. See "China dismisses Vietnam's sovereignty claim for South China Sea islands," *Xinhua,* 12 December 2012, available at http://news.xinhuanet.com/english/china/2014-12/12/c_133848818.htm

"Foreign Ministry Spokesperson Hong Lei's Regular Press Conference on September 22, 2011," Embassy of the People's Republic of China in the United States of America, 23 September 2011

"Foreign Ministry Spokesperson Jiang Yu's Regular Press Conference on September 15, 2011," Embassy of the People's Republic of China in The Republic of Kenya, 16 September 2011

"Foreign Ministry Spokesperson Hong Lei's Regular Press Conference on October 28, 2014," Permanent Mission of the People's Republic of China to the UN, 28 October 2014

"China dismisses recent tension in South China Sea as "old tricks" ,*Xinhuanet,* 26 May 2015 "Core interests at heart of new US ties," *Xinhuanet,* 20 May 2013

Wang Qian and Zhang Yunbi, "Xi vows to protect maritime interests," *China Daily,* 1 August 2013 "Transcript of the Joint Media Interaction of External Affairs Minister of India and Foreign Minister of Indonesia," Ministry of

External Affairs: Government of India, 27 July 2012

Also see, "India-China competition be in agreed strategic framework: SM Krishna," *The Economic Times*, 10 February 2012 (accessed on 25 June 2015)

see Anupama Airy and Jayanth Jacob, "China objects to oil hunt, India says back off," *Hindustan Times,*15 September 2011

"Transcript of media Interaction of External Affairs Minister following the conclusion of the plenary session of the ASEAN-India Commemorative Summit 2012," Media Centre, Ministry of External Affairs: Government of India, 20 December 2012

"Dispute over Islands in South China Sea," Lok Sabha Unstarred Question No. 563, Answered on 26 November 2014, Parliament Q & A, Ministry of External Affairs, Government of India

"Foreign Ministry Spokesperson Hua Chunying's Regular Press Conference on June 1, 2015," Ministry of Foreign Affairs of the People's Republic of China, 1 June 2015 "Foreign Ministry Spokesperson Hong Lei's Regular Press Conference on April 20, 2015," Ministry of Foreign Affairs of the People's Republic of China, 20 April 2015 .Sangkuk Lee, "China's 'Three Warfares': Origins, Applications, and Organizations," *The Journal of Strategic Studies*, vol. 37, no. 2, 2014, pp. 198-221

Guo Renjie, "Silk Road Fund makes initial $1.65b investment," *China Military Online*, April 20, 2015

Also see, "China makes multibillion-dollar down-payment on Silk Road Plans," *CHINAREALTIME,*21 April 2015

Ben Dolven, Jennifer K. Elsea, Susan V. Lawrence, Ronald O'Rourke and Ian E. Rinehart, "Chinese Land Reclamation in the South China Sea: Implications and Policy Options," Congressional Research Service Report, 16 June 2015

Also see "China to complete land reclamation of construction on some Nansha Islands soon," *Xinhuanet*, 16 June 2015

"China-Pak 'Boundary Agreement' Illegal: India", *Outlook*, 15 July 2009 (accessed on 22 June 2015); "Chinese Activities on Border," *Press Information Bureau: Ministry of Defense, Government of India*, 3 September 2012 (accessed on 22 June 2015)

Also see "Boundary Agreement between China and Pakistan, 2 March, 1963," *Pakistan Horizon,* Pakistan Institute of International Affairs, vol.16, No. 2, second quarter, 1963, pp. 177-182

"Joint Statement between the India and China during Prime Minister's visit to China," Press Information Bureau: Government of India: Prime Minister's Office, 15 May 2015

See One Belt One Road' initiative http://www.frontline.in/world-affairs/one-belt-one-road-initiative/article7098506.ece

See India opposed to China's One-Belt-One-Road available at http://www.deccanherald.com/content/532353/india-opposed-chinas-one-belt.html accessed on 4th March 2015

Also see What China's One Belt and One Road Strategy Means for India, Asia and the World *The Wire* at http://thewire.in/2015/10/09/what-chinas-one-belt-and-one-road-strategy-means-for-india-asia-and-the-world-12532/ accessed on 4th March 2015

4

Maritime Silk Road: An Indian Perspective

MH Rajesh

The *Belt and Road Initiative* (BRI) also called the *One Belt One Road* (OBOR) by China has attracted the attention of scholars and statesmen alike. Converting the recall value of the Ancient Silk Road, China has proposed a Sino centric idea of physical networks spanning continents and oceans. Apart from its physical vastness, the idea spans across a gamut of domains, from economics to culture. Physically, the Belt and Road Initiative has two segments. To the North is the land Route that cuts across Eurasia, called the Silk Road Economic Belt (SREB). To the South there is the sea route called Maritime Silk Road (MSR), commencing in the Chinese Coast passing through South East Asia into Indian Ocean touching several ports en route before terminating in Europe. This chapter will try to examine the historic premise, economic rationale, and dynamics of maritime transportation, geopolitical implications and responses to the Maritime Silk Road idea. The chapter will also examine areas of concerns and possible areas of convergence between India and China regarding One Belt One Road.

Historical Overview

It was Western demand for riches of Asia like China's silk and India's spice that inspired the vast network of roads and ports across Eurasia and Indian Ocean. Silk and spice were light, highly valued and were non-perishable making them ideal drivers of global commerce. During that phase of history, India and China together shared over 80% of global GDP[1]. World is again reaching a point of time when Asia is coming to its centre stage. The routes existed from 200BC to around 1500AD and came to be collectively called the Silk Route. The credit for the nomenclature of these routes as *Silk Route* goes to Ferdinand Richtofen, a German Geographer who published his work in 1877 after extensive exploration of this region. This ancient route weakened due to a tumultuous power shift along its alignment when the Ottoman Empire displaced the Byzantine Empire. This forced the western world to discover a direct sea route to India, being a destination as well as a significant transit hub, reduced the relevance of this network after 1500AD[2].The southern maritime route, the predecessor of present Maritime Silk Road offered far less terrestrial friction, could carry larger loads and faced lesser political uncertainties. It was also more multimodal, where predictable monsoon winds aided sea based transportation across Indian Ocean. The oceanic route handed goods over to a contiguous overland route which traversed across Egypt, onwards to Mediterranean coast. Across the Mediterranean, maritime mode clutched in again. The ease, economy of scale and multimodality, remains a key factor in Maritime Transportation. Till date 90% of global trade in volume is being carried via sea and therefore maritime transportation plays a significant role in global prosperity and growth.

Contemporary Silk Route

It was in October 2013, during a visit by Chinese President Xi Jinping[3]to Indonesia that the 21 Century Maritime Silk Road was announced. The location was significant; as Indonesia, the archipelagic nation is strategically located on the Maritime Silk Road. The exact contours of the Maritime Silk Road were released 18 months later through a Vision document in March 2015 on the side-lines of Boao Forum (the Asian equivalent of Davos), where leaders from industry and corporates meet informally[4]. The vision document is an omnibus document that covers a wide gamut of infrastructure, trade and finance to culture and education, to list only a few of them. The vision on the paper has been broad and its physical scope large. The vision document states that *"the 21st-Century Maritime Silk Road is designed to go from China's coast to Europe through the South China Sea and the Indian Ocean in one route, and from China's coast through the South China Sea to the South Pacific in the other"*. The two specific areas where India was directly affected and involved in OBOR were the Bangladesh--China-India-Myanmar Corridor (BCIM) and the China-Pakistan Economic Corridor (CPEC). Both these sub constructs have been described as 'closely related' to the One Belt One Road idea. An analysis of vision document indicated that the One Belt One Road was an open ended project in scope and participation. It articulated the contours in a broad manner without too much specifics. It connected most present projects, multilateral and bilateral organisations that involved China. The overall impression that the vision document gave out was that it was a process of re-branding and interweaving of what China was doing already or its future engagements in a variety of domains under one single umbrella giving Chinese economic and foreign policy engagement a new direction.

OBOR's Economic Perspective

The One Belt One Road vision document makes a direct reference to the 2008 global financial crisis highlighting the effect and lessons learned from that crisis[5]. The crisis not only exposed the weakness of the existing global economic structure, but also deeply affected China, which depended on a Foreign Direct Investment-Manufacture-Export model. Such a model of growth becomes unviable when an economy grows and leads to rising incomes. As China's economy grew, it reached that growth phase where it would have fallen into what some economists call the 'middle income trap 'where such a model is unviable. This resulted in slowing of growth, to what is known as the 'new normal', leading to search for a different model. The resultant idea it appears, is the One Belt One Road which essentially is integration of Chinese Economy with other economies, and the shifting of low end manufacturing to these economies. Such a construct allows China to focus on high technology manufacture scaling itself up the value chain thereby avoiding the "middle income trap". Transportation networks, infrastructure, capital and capacity were prerequisites for that idea. With the largest foreign exchange reserves and idling infrastructure capacity, China is in an ideal position to carry out such a construct. This is the trajectory that most Asian Tiger economies too have followed when they shifted manufacturing to China, at a certain point of their growth. This in a nutshell is understood as the economic rationale behind One Belt One Road. The argument is that if countries are to be coupled economically, there also needs to be structured studies on how new model can be mutually beneficial for both nations. Economists from both nations need to jointly examine the viability in the context of present trade imbalances.

Transportation Perspective

Connectivity between global economies is facilitated by a complex transportation system over air land and sea. Since the One Belt One Road is focusing on networks where transportation modes play a major role, a comparison between modes of transportation is in order. On land there are options of road, rail and pipelines, whereas over sea there are options of ships and pipelines. The cost of each mode varies and can go as high as 60% of the cost of product in cases like Liquefied Natural Gas. A modern container ship carries 18000 twenty feet containers, which if lined up will be 100 kilometers long. Possibilities of such economies of scale tilt the balance heavily in favor of the maritime transport. The economics of road, rail and maritime transport is best understood by a graph (Fig 4.1) from the book *Geography of Transport Systems* by Jean Paul Rodrigues. On the X axis, we have distances and on Y axis we have costs. The value of D1 is between 500-750 km and D2 is approximately 1500 km. The graphs C1, C2 and C3 indicate road, rail and marine modes. The commencing points of C1, C2, C3 shows the terminal costs, which shows that the terminal costs or costs incurred in infrastructure and handling at terminals are highest for maritime(C3), followed by rail(C2), whereas road is the cheapest(C1).

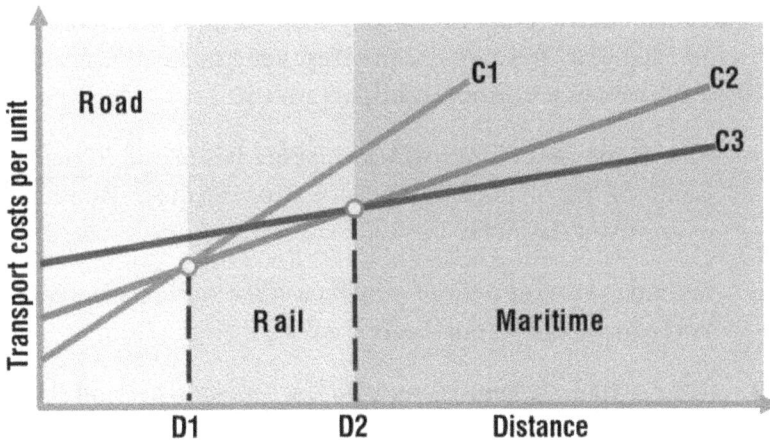

Fig. 4.1 Graph credit Geography of Transport Systems[6]

Simplifying the transportation debate to Land vs Sea mode based on costs alone can be highly misleading. Even though the two modes may appear to be competing with each other, in reality, the sea and land modes of networks are highly complementary. In the world of multimodal transport driven by containerization, one physical network cannot survive without another. Ships and oceans provide economy of scale between continents, whereas land modes provide last mile delivery. Without continental networks to hinterlands, the maritime network will be idle. Therefore, the Maritime Silk Road and Silk Road Economic Belt are viewed as highly complementary and interdependent constructs.

A Maritime Economic Perspective

There are certain maritime trends significant to networks that need to be discussed in context. Martin Stopford, one of the foremost analysts of Maritime Economics, has identified the **west line**, which is a fictional line that depicts the shift of centres of maritime activity across the globe in history. The 'centre' commenced five thousand years ago from Indian Ocean[7]. Today it has traversed three fourths of the globe and is hypothetically located in East Asia. The future progression of this line is westwards, to the Indian Ocean, where the centre of maritime economy will eventually shift. That six out of seven corridors planned in the One Belt One Road go westwards shows that the thrust is along the grain of 'West Line'. India too is setting the stage for the shift with 'Sagarmala', its own internal initiative. Stopford, the doyen of Maritime Transport after of analysis of 5000 years trajectory of the West line lists three major lessons which are relevant to a maritime transport system.

- First is the central part which shipping has played in the global economy. The locus of West line has also been the economic center of gravity of the globe.

- Second, is that the *basic of economics of the maritime business have not changed all that much over the years.*

- Third is that, *shipping prospers during periods of political stability*[8]. The relevance of security to shipping has also been highlighted by Jean Paul Rodrigues, another prominent scholar of transportation[9].

Maritime Economic Perspective as gleaned from westline indicates that shipping will always remain significant to global economy and political stability in international relations enables prosperous and peaceful shipping.

Maritime Geographic Trends

Whilst west line explains chronological shifts, there are significant geographic trends of shipping. Since earth is a sphere, the shortest distance around the sphere is along a great circle like the equator. Therefore, equatorial circum-navigation route, serves as the main trunk route of the global shipping network. This east-west line that connects the Panama, Suez Canals and Malacca straits is ideally served by large ships that offer economy of scale. However, canal size poses a limitation. The recent increase of size of Panama Canal has made this option more viable. This trunk line connect ports that serve as 'hubs' from where 'spokes' - the North South pendulum routes and inter ocean pendulum routes - serve the outlying ports. Transportation to the hinterland with gateways and corridors through intermodal options becomes critical for regionalized ports to efficiently adapt to these wider geographic trends.[10] What the maritime silk route or an Indian port based development initiative, 'Sagarmala' has to achieve is an integration to this global pattern of maritime trade and has to complement that trend for success. [11]

Maritime Security Perspectives

Having examined the maritime perspective, it is necessary to discuss the security and geopolitics of Maritime Silk Road. Maritime Security or peace over maritime routes is a prerequisite for maritime commerce. This has been highlighted by the very history of Silk route and studies of the west line. Therefore, even when the overall rationale of One Belt One Road is justified economically, there have been debates whether One Belt One Road will limit itself to economy or whether it is a strategic initiative with security underlays. The historic trend has been that such an ambitious network will be accompanied by security collaterals even if it has not been articulated in the vision document. The Flag has invariably followed trade in History. They appear either in the form of alliances or direct military presence providing security guarantee. The Chinese Defence Whitepaper of 2015[12], which followed a month after One Belt One Road vision document, was therefore, of deep interest to analysts. The defence whitepaper indicated a greater thrust to protection of trade, sea-power and trans- theatre mobility, which supports this argument. It is important that protection doesn't spiral into new geopolitical tensions in the region. Therefore, 'confidence building measures' become important with neighbours. Peace and prosperity are key to mutual development. There is a requirement to progress and utilise the Bilateral Maritime Dialogue for greater trust building and transparency.

India's Response

The Indian position on the One Belt One Road initiative has been that it is China's national initiative with little negotiations with others[13]or a structured bilateral discussion[14]. There has also been a view that there is insufficient information regarding the idea[15]. They appear as valid views that require redressal for progress in the One Belt One Road. Despite such a view by India, closer examination reveals that several projects closely related to BRI/One Belt One Road like those in the Bangladesh, China, India, Myanmar Corridor (BCIM) are being jointly examined by parties including India and China[16].

India has also become a founding partner in Asian Infrastructure Investment Bank (AIIB) and New Development Bank (NDB) which according to the vision document comes within the financial framework of One Belt One Road. Therefore, despite differences, where common interests converge, there are partnerships between India and China and wherever there are gaps, there are ongoing negotiations.

Areas of Concerns and Divergence

There are also certain areas of concern and divergence between India and China which has a bearing on Maritime Silk Road. It is essential to understand them for cooperation.

- A major project related to One Belt One Road is the China Pakistan Economic Corridor (CPEC). This 46 bn US$ project connects Kashgar in Xinjiang with Gwadar in Indian Ocean. The CPEC passes through the Indian State of Kashmir illegally occupied by Pakistan[17]. This is a matter of grave concern to India which has been conveyed to China.

- India and China as neighhbours, have an unsettled border over which a war was fought in 1962 which affects public memories. Though, to both nation's credit, border has been tranquil and both nations are taking the settlement process forward through special representatives, there is no denying that this unsettled issue has a bearing on bilateral relations. Settling of border issue can increase trust between both nations.

- The third concern is regarding arms sales by China. It has two aspects, first is a quantitative aspect and another is the qualitative aspect.

- A closer examination of pattern of arm sales by China indicates that quantitatively 70% of China's arms sales occur in the three nations that are India's maritime neighbors[18]namely Pakistan, Myanmar and Bangladesh. That the Maritime Silk Road touches each of these states definitely leads to concerns if that strategy is entwined with economics.

- There is also the nature of these weapons. Sale of lethal platforms like submarines to fragile states in region has the potential to affect stability in Indian Ocean Region. Unlike other oceans, the maritime security in Indian Ocean Region is biased to non-traditional threats emerging from fragile states. The threats of piracy and terrorism have funneled into the sea from such states. It took 30 global navies, including India and China ten years to combat piracy which threatened global commerce. The naval need of this region is platforms that can aid security of trade. Sale of submarines therefore raises deep questions if strategy has ruled over regional stability, which is most essential for common prosperity.

- Even though protection of trade by own security or an alliance is deemed a legitimate aspiration, certain maritime developments have been of concern to India. The presence of Chinese submarines in the very nodes of the Maritime Silk Road- in Pakistan and in Sri Lanka, though legitimate, evokes questions if the Maritime Silk Road idea would limit itself to economics alone[19].

- In Indian Ocean Region, the greatest emerging threat to maritime commerce is from terrorism. Al Qaeda[20] almost took over a Pakistan navy frigate and ISIS[21] has attacked naval and merchant ships. One of the worst uses of the sea for terror happened in 2008 in India when Lashkar-e-Taiba carried out attack in its maritime capital, Mumbai. Recently, India's attempts to bring the perpetrator of terror to book were blocked by China in UN[22]. This happened because Pakistan, state sponsor of terror, managed to play the victim. Being two major nations in Asia and world, India and China have to fight terror together in letter and spirit without any other political factors affecting it.

Areas of Convergence

It is felt that these concerns and divergence do not prevent cooperation. Being the two oldest civilizations, neighbors as well as emerging powers of the world, there have been examples of cooperation even amidst divergence between India and China. Their economic cooperation in the formation of the New Development Bank (NDB)[23] and the Asian Infrastructure Investment Bank[24] (AIIB) are successful examples where both nations have already cooperated. Prolonged negotiations to address interests of both parties were key to successful cooperation in these examples. There are other areas where the Indian and Chinese interests can converge in the future under the ambit of One Belt One Road.

- *Sagarmala-* **Indian Ports Initiative**

  In Mar 2015, India launched the *Sagarmala* project[25], which is a port based development model to spur a new phase of growth. India's share of coastal shipping and inland waterways in the transportation segment is below the global optimum. In order to develop ports, adjacent zones and inland waterways India intends to spend US 10 bn[26]. With the infrastructure capacities available in China for building economic zones and ports this could be an area of convergence[27]. This infrastructural initiative can not only give opportunities to infrastructure companies, but also ensures better connectivity to new Indian markets.

- **Cooperation in Infrastructure Projects**

  Asia requires close to 10tn US$ worth investment in infrastructure in next 10 years to meet developmental requirements. From its part, India has been in the process of creating several regional transportation networks. Some of them can link up or act in concert with OBOR. They are,

  o A North-South access to Central Asia from the Iranian Port of Chahbahar, which has the potential to connect land locked Central Asia to sea.

- o The Turkmenistan-Afghanistan-Pakistan-India (TAPI) pipeline.

- o The trilateral highway between India-Myanmar and Thailand.

- **_Mausam_- Cultural Initiative**

The third is the Indian initiative named 'Mausam' which is a purely cultural and historical initiative. Mausam, which means season in Arabic, connected Maritime Asia by a predictable wind system, the _Monsoon_. It is this weather phenomenon that enabled the original maritime route. Since culture and history is part of One Belt One Road convergence can be explored in this domain.

- **Other Indian Projects**

Just as China is trying to transform its economic model from the Foreign Direct Investment-Manufacture-Export model to a model driven by domestic consumption and services sector, India is currently transforming itself deeply through several initiatives. Some of the initiatives could be complimentary and can serve both economies.

- o **Make in India**[28] is an initiative that gives a fillip to manufacturing is one of the flagship projects of the government. This aims to encourage the manufacturing segment to spur growth of Indian Economy. It ushers in Indian and foreign investors with hundred percent foreign investments in all segments except defense, space and media. Given that Indian products can be competitive in pricing, they can form an integral part of the value global value chain. India is turning to manufacture, just as China is reforming its manufacture based economic model. This potentially, can be an area of convergence.

- o **Digital India**[29] is an initiative improving for online infrastructure and by increasing Internet connectivity. Digital India program focuses on specific areas, namely Broadband Highways, Universal Access to Mobile Connectivity, Public Internet Access, e-Governance, Electronic Delivery of Services, Electronics Manufacturing, and Information Technology for Jobs. Each of these areas cuts across multiple domains of expertise which will require global partnerships leading to convergence and opportunities. China's hardware and India's software capabilities have the potential to be complimentary capabilities, which can be exploited.

o **Smart Cities** projects which seeks innovative ideas for city infrastructure[30]. Broadly, it includes 'smart' innovative solutions to streamline basic amenities such as water, electricity, waste management, mobility, e governance, education, health, security and housing. It envisages 'keel up' green field projects as well as 'smart' overlays to legacy infrastructure to develop a sustainable urban ecosystem. Given that China has tremendous experience in infrastructure, and is reviewing its growth model, there will be lessons to share in this field especially since effects on environment is deemed an important factor in "smart cities".

o **Skill India**[31] a program to increase the skill sets of citizens. Compared to developed nations India lacks skilled work force. This initiative aims to ensure that the young workforce is re-skilled for employment and entrepreneur ship. Chinese experience in skill building quickly could add value to Indian plans in skilling its populace.

o **Startup India** This is an initiative to prime and encourage the entrepreneurial ecosystem in India through funding and tax incentives. In this field too China's trajectory could be studied by India.

These transformations cover a wide swath of infrastructure and industry. It opens up prospects for partnerships with India from across the globe including China. Given the vast experience and expertise of China in the infrastructure, high technology areas, participation in these projects will be mutually beneficial for both nations.

Recommendations

With this chapter as background, the following recommendations are suggested:-

- The One Belt One Road is seen in India as a Chinese national initiative, whereas China positions it as an international initiative. Hence, there is a perception gap on One Belt One Road. If this gap is to be bridged there is a requirement for China to reach out and negotiate with India and, given the open and democratic nature of the polity, be seen to be doing so. This has been expressed by Indian officials in open forums.

- Whilst there are concerns, there is also a view in India that there are elements in One Belt One Road that are useful for India. Some areas like *Sagarmala* are areas of convergence and have been mentioned previously in the chapter. Once a *reach out* occurs, the convergences and divergences need to be deliberated by experts in both nations through a structured dialogue. There indeed is that trust deficit between nations, which needs to be bridged by constant engagement at all levels between both nations. One significant way to build trust is through military to military cooperation through joint exercises and inter-operability.

Conclusion

Historically, maritime routes provide economies of scale acting in concert with land networks. Therefore, the Silk Road Economic Belt and Maritime Silk Road are highly complementary constructs. It is true that there are geopolitical concerns regarding the One Belt One Road in India, but where Indian and Chinese interests converge, there is precedence of cooperation between these two nations. India and China are 'two major powers in the region and world' which have legitimate aspirations regarding their own futures. Given the constructive relations between the two neighbours, there is a need to mutually address the concerns and divergences as we capitalize the convergences for which sufficient statecraft exists within both nations. To cite Prime Minister Modi, '*successful revival of the ancient trade routes require not only physical connectivity and requisite infrastructure, but even more important, a climate of peace, stability, mutual trust and respect, support for mutual prosperity and free flow of commerce and ideas*'[32]. The key to cooperation therefore, remains trust building between both nations.

End Notes

1   "The Economic History of the Last 2000 Years: Part II - The Atlantic," accessed on November 11, 2015, http://www.theatlantic.com/business/archive/2012/06/the-economic-history-of-the-last-2000-years-part-ii/258762/.

2   "The Silk Road and Arab Sea Routes," accessed on July 30, 2015, http://people.hofstra.edu/geotrans/eng/ch2en/conc2en/silkroad.html.

3   "Chronology of China's Belt and Road Initiative - Xinhua | English.news.cn," accessed on July 30, 2015, http://news.xinhuanet.com/english/2015-03/28/c_134105435.htm.

4   "Vision and Actions on Jointly Building Silk Road Economic Belt and 21st-Century Maritime Silk Road," accessed on July 30, 2015, http://www.fmprc.gov.cn/mfa_eng/zxxx_662805/t1249618.shtml.

5   Ibid.

6   Jean-Paul Rodrigue, Claude Comtois, and Brian Slack, The Geography of Transport Systems, 3 edition (Abingdon, Oxon: Routledge, 2013).

7   Martin Stopford, Maritime Economics 3e, 3 edition (London ; New York: Routledge, 2008).

8   Ibid.

9   "Maritime Transportation: Drivers for the Shipping and Port Industries - Transport Research International Documentation - TRID," accessed on November 22, 2015, http://trid.trb.org/view.aspx?id=1085868#.

10   Dr PK Ghosh "Daunting Realities: Territorial Disputes and Shipping Challenges to China's Maritime Silk Road " has appeared in the *Global Asia Journal * Vol 10 No. 3 Fall 2015 .https://globalasia.org/article/daunting-realities-territorial-disputes-and-shipping-challenges-to-chinas-maritime-silk-road/

11   Ibid.

12   accessed on November 13, 2015, http://eng.mod.gov.cn/Database/WhitePapers/.

13   "India Wrinkle on China Silk," The Telegraph, accessed on August 2, 2015, http://www.telegraphindia.com/1150721/jsp/frontpage/story_32798.jsp.

14   "Transcript of Media Briefing by Foreign Secretary in Beijing on Prime Minister's Ongoing Visit to China (may 15, 2015)," accessed on November 22, 2015, http://www.mea.gov.in/search-result.htm?25245/Transcript+of+Media+Briefing+by+Foreign+Secretary+in+Beijing+on+Prime+Ministers+ongoing+visit+to+China+may+15+2015.

15   "India Okay with BCIM, Wants Details on China Maritime Silk Road - Timesofindia-Economictimes," accessed on November 13, 2015, http://

articles.economictimes.indiatimes.com/2014-06-30/news/50974672_1_
maritime-silk-road-msr-bcim.

16 "BCIM: Can India Be a Driving Force?," *The Diplomat*, accessed on November
    13, 2015, http://thediplomat.com/2015/01/bcim-can-india-be-a-driving-
    force/.

17 "Modi Told China, Pakistan Economic Corridor Unacceptable: Sushma,"
    accessed on November 13, 2015, http://www.business-standard.com/article/
    news-ians/modi-told-china-pakistan-economic-corridor-unacceptable-
    sushma-115053100668_1.html.

18 Calculated by author from "SIPRI Arms Transfers Database — Www.sipri.
    org," Page, accessed on November 13, 2015, http://www.sipri.org/databases/
    armstransfers.

19 "China, Sri Lanka, and the Maritime Great Game," *Foreign Policy*, accessed on
    November 13, 2015, https://foreignpolicy.com/2015/02/12/china-sri-lanka-
    and-the-maritime-great-game-silk-road-xi-port/.

20 Syed Shoaib Hasan, Saeed Shah, and Siobhan Gorman, "Al Qaeda Militants
    Tried to Seize Pakistan Navy Frigate," *Wall Street Journal*, September 16, 2014,
    sec. World, http://www.wsj.com/articles/al-qaeda-militants-tried-to-seize-
    pakistan-navy-frigate-1410884514.

21 Reuters, "Isis Affiliate Claims Responsibility for Rocket Attack on Egyptian
    Navy Ship," *The Guardian*, July 16, 2015, sec. World news, http://www.
    theguardian.com/world/2015/jul/16/egypt-rocket-attack-sinai-province-isis-
    navy-ship.

22 "China Blocks Bid for U.N. Action on Pak. over Lakhvi," *The Hindu*, June
    24, 2015, http://www.thehindu.com/news/national/china-blocks-bid-for-un-
    action-on-pak-over-lakhvi/article7347637.ece.

23 "BRICS Bank Opens for Business in China - IBNLive," accessed on November
    13, 2015, http://www.ibnlive.com/news/world/brics-bank-opens-for-
    business-in-china-1023400.html.

24 "India Joins Asian Infrastructure Investment Bank - The Times of India,"
    accessed on November 13, 2015, http://timesofindia.indiatimes.com/
    business/india-business/India-joins-Asian-Infrastructure-Investment-Bank/
    articleshow/47874916.cms.

25 "Sagarmala: Concept and Implementation towards Blue Revolution," accessed
    on August 20, 2015, http://pmindia.gov.in/en/news_updates/sagarmala-
    concept-and-implementation-towards-blue-revolution/.

26 "Sagarmala Project: Government to Spend Rs 70,000 Crore on 12 Major
    Ports, Says Nitin Gadkari - The Economic Times," accessed on November 11,
    2015, http://economictimes.indiatimes.com/news/economy/infrastructure/
    sagarmala-project-government-to-spend-rs-70000-crore-on-12-major-
    ports-says-nitin-gadkari/articleshow/49229434.cms.

27 "Keynote Address by Prime Minister at India-China Business Forum in Shanghai (May 16, 2015)," accessed on November 22, 2015, http://mea.gov.in/ Speeches-Statements.htm?dtl/25247/Keynote_Address_by_Prime_Minister_ at_IndiaChina_Business_Forum_in_Shanghai_May_16_2015.

28 "Home - Make In India," accessed on November 13, 2015, http://www. makeinindia.com/home.

29 "Digital India | MyGov.in," accessed on November 13, 2015, https://mygov.in/ group/digital-india/.

30 "SmartCities.gov.in," accessed on November 13, 2015, http://smartcities.gov. in/.

31 "Skill India Portal," accessed on November 13, 2015, http://skillindia.gov.in/.

32 "Transcript of Prime Minister's Interaction with Chinese Media Organizations," accessed on November 22, 2015, http://mea.gov.in/interviews. htm?dtl/24011/Transcript_of_Prime_Ministers_Interaction_with_Chinese_ media_organizations.

References

"BCIM: Can India Be a Driving Force?" *The Diplomat.*Accessed on November 13, 2015. http://thediplomat.com/2015/01/bcim-can-india-be-a-driving-force/.

"BRICS Bank Opens for Business in China - IBNLive."Accessed on November 13, 2015. http://www.ibnlive.com/news/world/brics-bank-opens-for-business- in-china-1023400.html.

"China Blocks Bid for U.N. Action on Pak. over Lakhvi." *The Hindu*. June 24, 2015. http://www.thehindu.com/news/national/china-blocks-bid-for-un-action- on-pak-over-lakhvi/article7347637.ece.

"China, Sri Lanka, and the Maritime Great Game."*Foreign Policy.*Accessed on November 13, 2015. https://foreignpolicy.com/2015/02/12/china-sri-lanka- and-the-maritime-great-game-silk-road-xi-port/.

"Chronology of China's Belt and Road Initiative - Xinhua | English.news. cn."Accessed on July 30, 2015. http://news.xinhuanet.com/english/2015- 03/28/c_134105435.htm.

"Digital India | MyGov.in."Accessed on November 13, 2015. https://mygov.in/ group/digital-india/.

Hasan, Syed Shoaib, Saeed Shah, and Siobhan Gorman. "Al Qaeda Militants Tried to Seize Pakistan Navy Frigate." *Wall Street Journal*, September 16, 2014, sec. World. http://www.wsj.com/articles/al-qaeda-militants-tried-to-seize-pakistan-navy-frigate-1410884514.

"Home - Make In India." Accessed on November 13, 2015. http://www.makeinindia.com/home.

"India Joins Asian Infrastructure Investment Bank - The Times of India." Accessed on November 13, 2015. http://timesofindia.indiatimes.com/business/india-business/India-joins-Asian-Infrastructure-Investment-Bank/articleshow/47874916.cms.

"India Okay with BCIM, Wants Details on China Maritime Silk Road - Timesofindia-Economictimes."Accessed on November 13, 2015. http://articles.economictimes.indiatimes.com/2014-06-30/news/50974672_1_maritime-silk-road-msr-bcim.

"India Wrinkle on China Silk."*The Telegraph*.Accessed on August 2, 2015. http://www.telegraphindia.com/1150721/jsp/frontpage/story_32798.jsp.

"Keynote Address by Prime Minister at India-China Business Forum in Shanghai (May 16, 2015)." Accessed on November 22, 2015. http://mea.gov.in/Speeches-Statements.htm?dtl/25247/Keynote_Address_by_Prime_Minister_at_IndiaChina_Business_Forum_in_Shanghai_May_16_2015.

"Maritime Transportation: Drivers for the Shipping and Port Industries - Transport Research International Documentation - TRID." Accessed on November 22, 2015. http://trid.trb.org/view.aspx?id=1085868#.

"Modi Told China, Pakistan Economic Corridor Unacceptable: Sushma." Accessed on November 13, 2015. http://www.business-standard.com/article/news-ians/modi-told-china-pakistan-economic-corridor-unacceptable-sushma-115053100668_1.html.

Reuters. "Isis Affiliate Claims Responsibility for Rocket Attack on Egyptian Navy Ship."*The Guardian*, July 16, 2015, sec. World news. http://www.theguardian.com/world/2015/jul/16/egypt-rocket-attack-sinai-province-isis-navy-ship.

Rodrigue, Jean-Paul, Claude Comtois, and Brian Slack.*The Geography of Transport Systems*. 3 edition. Abingdon, Oxon: Routledge, 2013.

"Sagarmala Project: Government to Spend Rs 70,000 Crore on 12 Major Ports, Says Nitin Gadkari - The Economic Times." Accessed on November 11,

2015. http://economictimes.indiatimes.com/news/economy/infrastructure/ sagarmala-project-government-to-spend-rs-70000-crore-on-12-major-ports-says-nitin-gadkari/articleshow/49229434.cms.

"Sagarmala: Concept and Implementation towards Blue Revolution."says, Dr Arul Anthony Joseph. Accessed on August 20, 2015. http://pmindia.gov.in/ en/news_updates/sagarmala-concept-and-implementation-towards-blue-revolution/.

"SIPRI Arms Transfers Database — Www.sipri.org."Page.Accessed on November 13, 2015. http://www.sipri.org/databases/armstransfers.

"Skill India Portal."Accessed on November 13, 2015. http://skillindia.gov.in/.

"SmartCities.gov.in."Accessed on November 13, 2015. http://smartcities.gov.in/.

Stopford, Martin. *Maritime Economics 3e.* 3 edition. London ; New York: Routledge, 2008.

"The Economic History of the Last 2000 Years: Part II - The Atlantic." Accessed on November 11, 2015. http://www.theatlantic.com/business/archive/2012/06/ the-economic-history-of-the-last-2000-years-part-ii/258762/.

"The Silk Road and Arab Sea Routes."Accessed on July 30, 2015. http://people. hofstra.edu/geotrans/eng/ch2en/conc2en/silkroad.html.

"Transcript of Media Briefing by Foreign Secretary in Beijing on Prime Minister's Ongoing Visit to China (may 15, 2015)." Accessed on November 22, 2015. http://www.mea.gov.in/search-result.htm?25245/Transcript+of+Media+Brie fing+by+Foreign+Secretary+in+Beijing+on+Prime+Ministers+ongoing+vis it+to+China+may+15+2015.

"Transcript of Prime Minister's Interaction with Chinese Media Organizations."Accessed on November 22, 2015. http://mea.gov.in/interviews. htm?dtl/24011/Transcript_of_Prime_Ministers_Interaction_with_Chinese_ media_organizations.

"Vision and Actions on Jointly Building Silk Road Economic Belt and 21st-Century Maritime Silk Road."Accessed on July 30, 2015. http://www.fmprc. gov.cn/mfa_eng/zxxx_662805/t1249618.shtml.

Accessed November 13, 2015. http://eng.mod.gov.cn/Database/WhitePapers/.

Conclusion

Nivedita Das Kundu & MH Rajesh

The United Services Institution of India (USI), New Delhi and Sichuan University (SCU) Chengdu, under the scope of a MoU conducted joint research projects on the topic that has dominated the discourse on China across the globe and in the region- the 'One Belt One Road Initiative', (OBOR). Under its ambit, two Indian and two Chinese Scholars conducted the study. The Chinese Scholars has enunciated their perspectives on OBOR positioning it as a Chinese global initiative. The Indian Scholars divided their research based on geography with either of them researching into Continental (the Silk Road Economic Belt and 21st Century Maritime Silk Road) and Maritime (21st Century Maritime Silk Road) aspects of OBOR. The outcome of the joint research is produced in one volume, giving two separate perspectives about this topical subject. Beyond the granularities of this contemporary project, the joint research also obliquely brought the overall nature of this significant bilateral relation. The process of joint research involved presenting these papers in the respective institutions jointly.

Global Economies have evolved over natural connectivity networks that enabled exchanges through the ages. The Silk and Spice routes were two such legacy networks that spanned across Eurasia and the Maritime World of Indo-Pacific. If it was predictable monsoons across the oceans that enabled East-West Trade in Southern portion, it was the well-established caravan routes that traversed the plains and passes networking the northern continental land mass. Both networks complimented each other. History indicates that a favourable political system has always been a pre-requisite even in those trade networks. As one of the Chapters in this volume has alluded, it was the Ottoman's displacement of Eastern Roman Empire that motivated the age of maritime exploration. That political event disturbed and eventually displaced the land routes. Hence, geo-economic networks and geo-politics have historically shared a linkage between each other. This lesson is well known both in India and China which have shared several similarities in their history. It was trade that lead to political subjugation and even colonialism of either nations. One such milder version is of Chinese Admiral Zheng he who influenced a regime change in Srilanka during his forays in Indian Ocean. Therefore, one can expect as a basic tenet that trade networks are intrinsically political in nature. The question then becomes of creatively serving the purpose of prosperity without networks running aground on shoals of geopolitics. That is the challenge of the statesmen if sustenance of networks is important.

The 'One Belt one Road', is a resurrection of that East-West Eurasian network of yore- albeit in a modern manner. Marshalling the immense idle capital, skills and resources infusing the state of the art technology available at Chinese command today, this appears inspired by that history. The hardware, one must concede, is highly plausible given Chinese capacity and reputation for it. However, its 'software'- demands nuanced state craft and building genuine good will borne of trust. The challenge therefore, is how to fashion that software using contemporary understanding of politics, law, customs and trade deficits to mitigate the seamier sides that have shown up. Even perceptions require redressal when such an ambitious plan is laid out.

India's response to OBOR as reflected by the scholars in this volume has been cautious. The rationale behind this caution appears the concern about the network's umbilical to politics. One of the concerns voiced has been if these new networks are leading Asia into old problems. Hence, scholars have examined some scopes for a common meeting ground.

Infrastructure networks are essential for prosperity and development. The reality is that it is an economic necessity today for every nation including China, to create global value chains. There is simply no dearth of laws from the Sarnoff's, Metcalf's or the Reed's that reiterate the evolving power of networks across domains of industry. The foundation of all these networks is basic infrastructure like roads, rails, power and communication lines. The regional and national competencies that add value to the product or service chain today crosses borders. Enterprises have become truly global with transnational, distributed business architectures that optimise production. Governments have to create an infrastructure that commensurate with such a transnational value chain. Just as OBOR, India has also laid out its plans for networks like the Trilateral Highway connecting India, Myanmar and Thailand, North South transport Corridor from Mumbai to Chahbahar connecting Central Asia to Arabian Sea, another connectivity project is the Bangladesh and Bhutan- India- Nepal Corridor (BBIN). This is apart from its own internal port development initiatives like the *Sagarmala*.

These networks, for which billions are being invested along with the Chinese OBOR, have the potential to transform Asia, if synergised well. It could take millions out of poverty and can serve as triggers for regional development. However, synergising these networks requires nuanced statecraft, deeper commercial, diplomatic, economic engagements. As far as OBOR is concerned India's position has been such that there have been no bilateral negotiations held between India and China specific to OBOR initiave. Needless to say, the chequered histories of bilateral relations have worked as a backdrop to this position.

Just as the world cannot ignore India or China, India and China also cannot ignore each other and prosper. India is a very large market that cannot be avoided by any country. OBOR, if it is about economics, will eventually have to deal with India given its size, growth rates, demography, and geographic location. Similarly, India will have to deal with China given the latter's experience besides the proportionally larger heft.

At its simplest level, if current positions do not yield a middle meeting ground, there has to be a relook at respective positions with a realistic prism. China will have to address some of India's concern, especially of a bilateral negotiation, which is in fact the lowest hanging fruit of all. Similarly India will have to look pragmatically at the benefits of synergising its plans with OBOR, if not of joining OBOR in a win-win manner. Asian landscape is badly in need of investments in infrastructure. These networks must lead to prosperity and peace and not lead to tensions. History shows us that the Silk and Spice routes intermingled well in the past and yet, India and China prospered well. It would be a travesty if despite civilizational accretion over centuries, that feat can't be repeated. It is hoped that the study conducted by the four scholars on this significant topic, though not comprehensive, can aid that process.

Vision and Actions on Jointly Building Silk Road Economic Belt and 21st-Century Maritime Silk Road

2015/03/28

Issued by the National Development and Reform Commission, Ministry of Foreign Affairs, and Ministry of Commerce of the People's Republic of China, with State Council authorization

March 2015

Contents

Preface

More than two millennia ago the diligent and courageous people of Eurasia explored and opened up several routes of trade and cultural exchanges that linked the major civilizations of Asia, Europe and Africa, collectively called the Silk Road by later generations. For thousands of years, the Silk Road Spirit – "peace and cooperation, openness and inclusiveness, mutual learning and mutual benefit" – has been passed from generation to generation, promoted the progress of human civilization, and contributed greatly to the prosperity and development of the countries along the Silk

Road. Symbolizing communication and cooperation between the East and the West, the Silk Road Spirit is a historic and cultural heritage shared by all countries around the world.

In the 21st century, a new era marked by the theme of peace, development, cooperation and mutual benefit, it is all the more important for us to carry on the Silk Road Spirit in face of the weak recovery of the global economy, and complex international and regional situations.

When Chinese President Xi Jinping visited Central Asia and Southeast Asia in September and October of 2013, he raised the initiative of jointly building the Silk Road Economic Belt and the 21st-Century Maritime Silk Road (hereinafter referred to as the Belt and Road), which have attracted close attention from all over the world. At the China-ASEAN Expo in 2013, Chinese Premier Li Keqiang emphasized the need to build the Maritime Silk Road oriented towards ASEAN, and to create strategic propellers for hinterland development. Accelerating the building of the Belt and Road can help promote the economic prosperity of the countries along the Belt and Road and regional economic cooperation, strengthen exchanges and mutual learning between different civilizations, and promote world peace and development. It is a great undertaking that will benefit people around the world.

The Belt and Road Initiative is a systematic project, which should be jointly built through consultation to meet the interests of all, and efforts should be made to integrate the development strategies of the countries along the Belt and Road. The Chinese government has drafted and published the Vision and Actions on Jointly Building Silk Road Economic Belt and 21st-Century Maritime Silk Road to promote the implementation of the Initiative, instill vigor and vitality into the ancient Silk Road, connect Asian, European and African countries more closely and promote mutually beneficial cooperation to a new high and in new forms.

I. Background

Complex and profound changes are taking place in the world. The underlying impact of the international financial crisis keeps emerging; the world economy is recovering slowly, and global development is uneven; the international trade and investment landscape and rules for multilateral trade and investment are undergoing major adjustments; and countries still face big challenges to their development.

The initiative to jointly build the Belt and Road, embracing the trend towards a multipolar world, economic globalization, cultural diversity and greater IT application, is designed to uphold the global free trade regime and the open world economy in the spirit of open regional cooperation. It is aimed at promoting orderly and free flow of economic factors, highly efficient allocation of resources and deep integration of markets; encouraging the countries along the Belt and Road to achieve economic policy coordination and carry out broader and more in-depth regional cooperation of higher standards; and jointly creating an open, inclusive and balanced regional economic cooperation architecture that benefits all. Jointly building the Belt and Road is in the interests of the world community. Reflecting the common ideals and pursuit of human societies, it is a positive endeavor to seek new models of international cooperation and global governance, and will inject new positive energy into world peace and development.

The Belt and Road Initiative aims to promote the connectivity of Asian, European and African continents and their adjacent seas, establish and strengthen partnerships among the countries along the Belt and Road, set up all-dimensional, multi-tiered and composite connectivity networks, and realize diversified, independent, balanced and sustainable development in these countries. The connectivity projects of the Initiative will help align and coordinate the development strategies of the countries along the Belt and Road, tap market potential in this region, promote investment and consumption, create demands and job opportunities, enhance people-to-people and cultural exchanges, and mutual learning among the peoples of the relevant countries, and enable them to understand, trust and respect each other and live in harmony, peace and prosperity.

China's economy is closely connected with the world economy. China will stay committed to the basic policy of opening-up, build a new pattern of all-round opening-up, and integrate itself deeper into the world economic system. The Initiative will enable China to further expand and deepen its opening-up, and to strengthen its mutually beneficial cooperation with countries in Asia, Europe and Africa and the rest of the world. China is committed to shouldering more responsibilities and obligations within its capabilities, and making greater contributions to the peace and development of mankind.

II. Principles

The Belt and Road Initiative is in line with the purposes and principles of the UN Charter. It upholds the Five Principles of Peaceful Coexistence: mutual respect for each other's sovereignty and territorial integrity, mutual non-aggression, mutual non-interference in each other's internal affairs, equality and mutual benefit, and peaceful coexistence.

The Initiative is open for cooperation. It covers, but is not limited to, the area of the ancient Silk Road. It is open to all countries, and international and regional organizations for engagement, so that the results of the concerted efforts will benefit wider areas.

The Initiative is harmonious and inclusive. It advocates tolerance among civilizations, respects the paths and modes of development chosen by different countries, and supports dialogues among different civilizations on the principles of seeking common ground while shelving differences and drawing on each other's strengths, so that all countries can coexist in peace for common prosperity.

The Initiative follows market operation. It will abide by market rules and international norms, give play to the decisive role of the market in resource allocation and the primary role of enterprises, and let the governments perform their due functions.

The Initiative seeks mutual benefit. It accommodates the interests and concerns of all parties involved, and seeks a conjunction of interests and the "biggest common denominator" for cooperation so as to give full play to the wisdom and creativity, strengths and potentials of all parties.

III. Framework

The Belt and Road Initiative is a way for win-win cooperation that promotes common development and prosperity and a road towards peace and friendship by enhancing mutual understanding and trust, and strengthening all-round exchanges. The Chinese government advocates peace and cooperation, openness and inclusiveness, mutual learning and mutual benefit. It promotes practical cooperation in all fields, and works to build a community of shared interests, destiny and responsibility featuring mutual political trust, economic integration and cultural inclusiveness.

The Belt and Road run through the continents of Asia, Europe and Africa, connecting the vibrant East Asia economic circle at one end and developed European economic circle at the other, and encompassing countries with huge potential for economic development. The Silk Road Economic Belt focuses on bringing together China, Central Asia, Russia and Europe (the Baltic); linking China with the Persian Gulf and the Mediterranean Sea through Central Asia and West Asia; and connecting China with Southeast Asia, South Asia and the Indian Ocean. The 21st-Century Maritime Silk Road is designed to go from China's coast to Europe through the South China Sea and the Indian Ocean in one route, and from China's coast through the South China Sea to the South Pacific in the other.

On land, the Initiative will focus on jointly building a new Eurasian Land Bridge and developing China-Mongolia-Russia, China-Central Asia-West Asia and China-Indochina Peninsula economic corridors by taking advantage of international transport routes, relying on core cities along the Belt and Road and using key economic industrial parks as cooperation platforms. At sea, the Initiative will focus on jointly building smooth, secure and efficient transport routes connecting major sea ports along the Belt and Road. The China-Pakistan Economic Corridor and the Bangladesh-China-India-Myanmar Economic Corridor are closely related to the Belt and Road Initiative, and therefore require closer cooperation and greater progress.

The Initiative is an ambitious economic vision of the opening-up of and cooperation among the countries along the Belt and Road. Countries should work in concert and move towards the objectives of mutual benefit and common security. To be specific, they need to improve the region's infrastructure, and put in place a secure and efficient network of land, sea and air passages, lifting their connectivity to a higher level; further enhance trade and investment facilitation, establish a network of free trade areas that meet high standards, maintain closer economic ties, and deepen political trust; enhance cultural exchanges; encourage different civilizations to learn from each other and flourish together; and promote mutual understanding, peace and friendship among people of all countries.

IV. Cooperation Priorities

Countries along the Belt and Road have their own resource advantages and their economies are mutually complementary. Therefore, there is a great potential and space for cooperation. They should promote policy coordination, facilities connectivity, unimpeded trade, financial integration and people-to-people bonds as their five major goals, and strengthen cooperation in the following key areas:

Policy coordination

Enhancing policy coordination is an important guarantee for implementing the Initiative. We should promote intergovernmental cooperation, build a multi-level intergovernmental macro policy exchange and communication mechanism, expand shared interests, enhance mutual political trust, and reach new cooperation consensus. Countries along the Belt and Road may fully coordinate their economic development strategies and policies, work out plans and measures for regional cooperation, negotiate to solve cooperation-related issues, and jointly provide policy support for the implementation of practical cooperation and large-scale projects.

Facilities connectivity

Facilities connectivity is a priority area for implementing the Initiative. On the basis of respecting each other's sovereignty and security concerns, countries along the Belt and Road should improve the connectivity of their infrastructure construction plans and technical standard systems, jointly push forward the construction of international trunk passageways, and form an infrastructure network connecting all sub-regions in Asia, and between Asia, Europe and Africa step by step. At the same time, efforts should be made to promote green and low-carbon infrastructure construction and operation management, taking into full account the impact of climate change on the construction.

With regard to transport infrastructure construction, we should focus on the key passageways, junctions and projects, and give priority to linking up unconnected road sections, removing transport bottlenecks, advancing road safety facilities and traffic management facilities and equipment, and improving road network connectivity. We should build a unified coordination mechanism for whole-course transportation, increase connectivity of customs clearance, reloading and multimodal transport between countries, and gradually formulate compatible and standard transport rules, so as to realize international transport facilitation. We should push forward port infrastructure construction, build smooth land-water transportation channels, and advance port cooperation; increase sea routes and the number of voyages, and enhance information technology cooperation in maritime logistics. We should expand and build platforms and mechanisms for comprehensive civil aviation cooperation, and quicken our pace in improving aviation infrastructure.

We should promote cooperation in the connectivity of energy infrastructure, work in concert to ensure the security of oil and gas pipelines and other transport routes, build cross-border power supply networks and power-transmission routes, and cooperate in regional power grid upgrading and transformation.

We should jointly advance the construction of cross-border optical cables and other communications trunk line networks, improve international communications connectivity, and create an Information Silk Road. We should build bilateral cross-border optical cable networks at a quicker pace, plan transcontinental submarine optical cable projects, and improve spatial (satellite) information passageways to expand information exchanges and cooperation.

Unimpeded trade

Investment and trade cooperation is a major task in building the Belt and Road. We should strive to improve investment and trade facilitation, and remove investment and trade barriers for the creation of a sound business environment within the region and in all related countries. We will discuss with countries and regions along the Belt and Road on opening free trade areas so as to unleash the potential for expanded cooperation.

Countries along the Belt and Road should enhance customs cooperation such as information exchange, mutual recognition of regulations, and mutual assistance in law enforcement; improve bilateral and multilateral cooperation in the fields of inspection and quarantine, certification and accreditation, standard measurement, and statistical information; and work to ensure that the WTO Trade Facilitation Agreement takes effect and is implemented. We should improve the customs clearance facilities of border ports, establish a "single-window" in border ports, reduce customs clearance costs, and improve customs clearance capability. We should increase cooperation in supply chain safety and convenience, improve the coordination of cross-border supervision procedures, promote online checking of inspection and quarantine certificates, and facilitate mutual recognition of Authorized Economic Operators. We should lower non-tariff barriers, jointly improve the transparency of technical trade measures, and enhance trade liberalization and facilitation.

We should expand trading areas, improve trade structure, explore new growth areas of trade, and promote trade balance. We should make innovations in our forms of trade, and develop cross-border e-commerce and other modern business models. A service trade support system should be set up to consolidate and expand conventional trade, and efforts to develop modern service trade should be strengthened. We should integrate investment and trade, and promote trade through investment.

We should speed up investment facilitation, eliminate investment barriers, and push forward negotiations on bilateral investment protection agreements and double taxation avoidance agreements to protect the lawful rights and interests of investors.

We should expand mutual investment areas, deepen cooperation in agriculture, forestry, animal husbandry and fisheries, agricultural machinery manufacturing and farm produce processing, and promote cooperation in marine-product farming, deep-sea fishing, aquatic product processing, seawater desalination, marine biopharmacy, ocean engineering technology, environmental protection industries, marine tourism and other fields. We should increase cooperation in the exploration and development of coal, oil, gas, metal minerals and other conventional energy sources; advance cooperation in hydropower, nuclear power, wind power, solar power and other clean, renewable energy sources; and promote cooperation in the processing and conversion of energy and resources at or near places where they are exploited, so as to create an integrated industrial chain of energy and resource cooperation. We should enhance cooperation in deep-processing technology, equipment and engineering services in the fields of energy and resources.

We should push forward cooperation in emerging industries. In accordance with the principles of mutual complementarity and mutual benefit, we should promote in-depth cooperation with other countries along the Belt and Road in new-generation information technology, biotechnology, new energy technology, new materials and other emerging industries, and establish entrepreneurial and investment cooperation mechanisms.

We should improve the division of labor and distribution of industrial chains by encouraging the entire industrial chain and related industries to develop in concert; establish R&D, production and marketing systems; and improve industrial supporting capacity and the overall competitiveness of regional industries. We should increase the openness of our service industry to each other to accelerate the development of regional service industries. We should explore a new mode of investment cooperation, working together to build all forms of industrial parks such as overseas economic and trade cooperation zones and cross-border economic cooperation zones, and promote industrial cluster development. We should promote ecological progress in conducting investment and trade, increase cooperation in conserving eco-environment, protecting biodiversity, and tackling climate change, and join hands to make the Silk Road an environment-friendly one.

We welcome companies from all countries to invest in China, and encourage Chinese enterprises to participate in infrastructure construction in other countries along the Belt and Road, and make industrial investments there. We support localized operation and management of Chinese companies to boost the local economy, increase local employment, improve local livelihood, and take social responsibilities in protecting local biodiversity and eco-environment.

Financial integration

Financial integration is an important underpinning for implementing the Belt and Road Initiative. We should deepen financial cooperation, and make more efforts in building a currency stability system, investment and financing system and credit information system in Asia. We should expand the scope and scale of bilateral currency swap and settlement with other countries along the Belt and Road, open and develop the bond market in Asia, make joint efforts to establish the Asian Infrastructure Investment Bank and BRICS New Development Bank, conduct negotiation among related parties on establishing Shanghai Cooperation Organization (SCO) financing institution, and set up and put into operation the Silk Road Fund as early as possible. We should strengthen practical cooperation of China-ASEAN Interbank Association and SCO Interbank Association, and carry out multilateral financial cooperation in the form of syndicated loans and bank credit. We will support the efforts of governments of the countries along the Belt and Road and their companies and financial institutions with good credit-rating to issue Renminbi bonds in China. Qualified Chinese financial institutions and companies are encouraged to issue bonds in both Renminbi and foreign currencies outside China, and use the funds thus collected in countries along the Belt and Road.

We should strengthen financial regulation cooperation, encourage the signing of MOUs on cooperation in bilateral financial regulation, and establish an efficient regulation coordination mechanism in the region. We should improve the system of risk response and crisis management, build a regional financial risk early-warning system, and create an exchange and cooperation mechanism of addressing cross-border risks and crisis. We should increase cross-border exchange and cooperation between credit investigation regulators, credit investigation institutions and credit rating institutions. We should give full play to the role of the Silk Road Fund and that of sovereign wealth funds of countries along the Belt and Road, and encourage commercial equity investment funds and private funds to participate in the construction of key projects of the Initiative.

People-to-people bond

People-to-people bond provides the public support for implementing the Initiative. We should carry forward the spirit of friendly cooperation of the Silk Road by promoting extensive cultural and academic exchanges, personnel exchanges and cooperation, media cooperation, youth and women exchanges and volunteer services, so as to win public support for deepening bilateral and multilateral cooperation.

We should send more students to each other's countries, and promote cooperation in jointly running schools. China provides 10,000 government scholarships to the countries along the Belt and Road every year. We should hold culture years, arts festivals, film festivals, TV weeks and book fairs in each other's countries; cooperate on the production and translation of fine films, radio and TV programs; and jointly apply for and protect World Cultural Heritage sites. We should also increase personnel exchange and cooperation between countries along the Belt and Road.

We should enhance cooperation in and expand the scale of tourism; hold tourism promotion weeks and publicity months in each other's countries; jointly create competitive international tourist routes and products with Silk Road features; and make it more convenient to apply for tourist visa in countries along the Belt and Road. We should push forward cooperation on the 21st-Century Maritime Silk Road cruise tourism program. We should carry out sports exchanges and support countries along the Belt and Road in their bid for hosting major international sports events.

We should strengthen cooperation with neighboring countries on epidemic information sharing, the exchange of prevention and treatment technologies and the training of medical professionals, and improve our capability to jointly address public health emergencies. We will provide medical assistance and emergency medical aid to relevant countries, and carry out practical cooperation in maternal and child health, disability rehabilitation, and major infectious diseases including AIDS, tuberculosis and malaria. We will also expand cooperation on traditional medicine.

We should increase our cooperation in science and technology, establish joint labs (or research centers), international technology transfer centers and maritime cooperation centers, promote sci-tech personnel exchanges, cooperate in tackling key sci-tech problems, and work together to improve sci-tech innovation capability.

We should integrate existing resources to expand and advance practical cooperation between countries along the Belt and Road on youth employment, entrepreneurship training, vocational skill development, social security management, public administration and management and in other areas of common interest.

We should give full play to the bridging role of communication between political parties and parliaments, and promote friendly exchanges between legislative bodies, major political parties and political organizations of countries along the Belt and Road. We should carry out exchanges and cooperation among cities, encourage major cities in these countries to become sister cities, focus on promoting practical cooperation, particularly cultural and people-to-people exchanges, and create more lively examples of cooperation. We welcome the think tanks in the countries along the Belt and Road to jointly conduct research and hold forums.

We should increase exchanges and cooperation between non-governmental organizations of countries along the Belt and Road, organize public interest activities concerning education, health care, poverty reduction, biodiversity and ecological protection for the benefit of the general public, and improve the production and living conditions of poverty-stricken areas along the Belt and Road. We should enhance international exchanges and cooperation on culture and media, and leverage the positive role of the Internet and new media tools to foster harmonious and friendly cultural environment and public opinion.

V. Cooperation Mechanisms

The world economic integration is accelerating and regional cooperation is on the upswing. China will take full advantage of the existing bilateral and multilateral cooperation mechanisms to push forward the building of the Belt and Road and to promote the development of regional cooperation.

We should strengthen bilateral cooperation, and promote comprehensive development of bilateral relations through multi-level and multi-channel communication and consultation. We should encourage the signing of cooperation MOUs or plans, and develop a number of bilateral cooperation pilot projects. We should establish and improve bilateral joint working mechanisms, and draw up implementation plans and roadmaps for advancing the Belt and Road Initiative. In addition, we should give full play to the existing bilateral mechanisms such as joint committee, mixed committee, coordinating committee, steering committee and management committee to coordinate and promote the implementation of cooperation projects.

We should enhance the role of multilateral cooperation mechanisms, make full use of existing mechanisms such as the Shanghai Cooperation Organization (SCO), ASEAN Plus China (10+1), Asia-Pacific Economic Cooperation (APEC), Asia-Europe Meeting (ASEM), Asia Cooperation Dialogue (ACD), Conference on Interaction and Confidence-Building Measures in Asia (CICA), China-Arab States Cooperation Forum (CASCF), China-Gulf Cooperation Council Strategic Dialogue, Greater Mekong Sub-region (GMS) Economic Cooperation, and Central Asia Regional Economic Cooperation (CAREC) to strengthen communication with relevant countries, and attract more countries and regions to participate in the Belt and Road Initiative.

We should continue to encourage the constructive role of the international forums and exhibitions at regional and sub-regional levels hosted by countries along the Belt and Road, as well as such platforms as Boao Forum for Asia, China-ASEAN Expo, China-Eurasia Expo, Euro-Asia Economic Forum, China International Fair for Investment and Trade, China-South Asia Expo, China-Arab States Expo, Western China International Fair, China-Russia Expo, and Qianhai Cooperation Forum. We should support the local authorities and general public of countries along the Belt and Road to explore the historical and cultural heritage of the Belt and Road, jointly hold investment, trade and cultural exchange activities, and ensure the success of the Silk Road (Dunhuang) International Culture Expo, Silk Road International Film Festival and Silk Road International Book Fair. We propose to set up an international summit forum on the Belt and Road Initiative.

VI. China's Regions in

Pursuing Opening-Up

In advancing the Belt and Road Initiative, China will fully leverage the comparative advantages of its various regions, adopt a proactive strategy of further opening-up, strengthen interaction and cooperation among the eastern, western and central regions, and comprehensively improve the openness of the Chinese economy.

Northwestern and northeastern regions. We should make good use of Xinjiang's geographic advantages and its role as a window of westward opening-up to deepen communication and cooperation with Central, South and West Asian countries, make it a key transportation, trade, logistics, culture, science and education center, and a core area on the Silk Road Economic Belt. We should give full scope to the economic and cultural strengths of Shaanxi and Gansu provinces and the ethnic and cultural advantages of the Ningxia Hui Autonomous Region and Qinghai Province, build Xi'an into a new focus of reform and opening-up in China's interior, speed up the development and opening-up of cities such as Lanzhou and Xining, and advance the building of the Ningxia Inland Opening-up Pilot Economic Zone with the goal of creating strategic channels, trade and logistics hubs and key bases for industrial and cultural exchanges opening to Central, South and West Asian countries. We should give full play to Inner Mongolia's proximity to Mongolia and Russia, improve the railway links connecting Heilongjiang Province with Russia and the regional railway network, strengthen cooperation between China's Heilongjiang, Jilin and Liaoning provinces and Russia's Far East region on sea-land multimodal transport, and advance the construction of an Eurasian high-speed transport corridor linking Beijing and Moscow with the goal of building key windows opening to the north.

Southwestern region. We should give full play to the unique advantage of Guangxi Zhuang Autonomous Region as a neighbor of ASEAN countries, speed up the opening-up and development of the Beibu Gulf Economic Zone and the Pearl River-Xijiang Economic Zone, build an international corridor opening to the ASEAN region, create new strategic anchors for the opening-up and development of the southwest and mid-south regions of China, and form an important gateway connecting the Silk Road Economic Belt and the 21st-Century Maritime Silk Road. We should make good use of the geographic advantage of Yunnan Province, advance the construction of an international transport corridor connecting China with neighboring countries, develop a new highlight of economic cooperation in the Greater Mekong Sub-region, and make the region a pivot of China's opening-up to South and Southeast Asia. We should promote the border trade and tourism and culture cooperation between Tibet Autonomous Region and neighboring countries such as Nepal.

Coastal regions, and Hong Kong, Macao and Taiwan. We should leverage the strengths of the Yangtze River Delta, Pearl River Delta, west coast of the Taiwan Straits, Bohai Rim, and other areas with economic zones boasting a high level of openness, robust economic strengths and strong catalytic role, speed up the development of the China (Shanghai) Pilot Free Trade Zone, and support Fujian Province in becoming a core area of the 21st-Century Maritime Silk Road. We should give full scope to the role of Qianhai (Shenzhen), Nansha (Guangzhou), Hengqin (Zhuhai) and Pingtan (Fujian) in opening-up and cooperation, deepen their cooperation with Hong Kong, Macao and Taiwan, and help to build the Guangdong-Hong Kong-Macao Big Bay Area. We should promote the development of the Zhejiang Marine Economy Development Demonstration Zone, Fujian Marine Economic Pilot Zone and Zhoushan Archipelago New Area, and further open Hainan Province as an international tourism island. We should strengthen the port construction of coastal cities such as Shanghai, Tianjin, Ningbo-Zhoushan, Guangzhou, Shenzhen, Zhanjiang, Shantou, Qingdao, Yantai, Dalian, Fuzhou, Xiamen, Quanzhou, Haikou and Sanya, and strengthen the functions of international hub airports such as Shanghai and Guangzhou. We should use opening-up to motivate these areas to carry out deeper reform, create new systems and mechanisms of open economy, step up scientific and technological innovation, develop new advantages for participating in and leading international cooperation and competition, and become the pace-setter and main force in the Belt and Road Initiative, particularly the building of the 21st-Century Maritime Silk Road. We should leverage the unique role of overseas Chinese and the Hong Kong and Macao Special Administrative Regions, and encourage them to participate in and contribute to the Belt and Road Initiative. We should also make proper arrangements for the Taiwan region to be part of this effort.

Inland regions. We should make use of the advantages of inland regions, including a vast landmass, rich human resources and a strong industrial foundation, focus on such key regions as the city clusters along the middle reaches of the Yangtze River, around Chengdu and Chongqing, in central Henan Province, around Hohhot, Baotou, Erdos and Yulin, and around Harbin and Changchun to propel regional interaction and cooperation and industrial concentration. We should build Chongqing into an important pivot for developing and opening up the western region, and make Chengdu, Zhengzhou, Wuhan, Changsha, Nanchang and Hefei leading areas of opening-up in the inland regions. We should accelerate cooperation between regions on the upper and middle reaches of the Yangtze River and their counterparts along Russia's Volga River. We should set up coordination mechanisms in terms of railway transport and port customs clearance for the China-Europe corridor, cultivate the brand of "China-Europe freight trains," and construct a cross-border transport corridor connecting the eastern, central and western regions. We should support inland cities such as Zhengzhou and Xi'an in building airports and international land ports, strengthen customs clearance cooperation between inland ports and ports in the coastal and border regions, and launch pilot e-commerce services for cross-border trade. We should optimize the layout of special customs oversight areas, develop new models of processing trade, and deepen industrial cooperation with countries along the Belt and Road.

VII. China in Action

For more than a year, the Chinese government has been actively promoting the building of the Belt and Road, enhancing communication and consultation and advancing practical cooperation with countries along the

Belt and Road, and introduced a series of policies and measures for early outcomes.

High-level guidance and facilitation. President Xi Jinping and Premier Li Keqiang have visited over 20 countries, attended the Dialogue on Strengthening Connectivity Partnership and the sixth ministerial conference of the China-Arab States Cooperation Forum, and met with leaders of relevant countries to discuss bilateral relations and regional development issues. They have used these opportunities to explain the rich contents and positive implications of the Belt and Road Initiative, and their efforts have helped bring about a broad consensus on the Belt and Road Initiative.

Signing cooperation framework. China has signed MOUs of cooperation on the joint development of the Belt and Road with some countries, and on regional cooperation and border cooperation and mid- and long-term development plans for economic and trade cooperation with some neighboring countries. It has proposed outlines of regional cooperation plans with some adjacent countries.

Promoting project cooperation. China has enhanced communication and consultation with countries along the Belt and Road, and promoted a number of key cooperation projects in the fields of infrastructure connectivity, industrial investment, resource development, economic and trade cooperation, financial cooperation, cultural exchanges, ecological protection and maritime cooperation where the conditions are right.

Improving policies and measures. The Chinese government will integrate its domestic resources to provide stronger policy support for the Initiative. It will facilitate the establishment of the Asian Infrastructure Investment Bank. China has proposed the Silk Road Fund, and the investment function of the China-Eurasia Economic Cooperation Fund will be reinforced. We will encourage bank card clearing institutions to conduct cross-border clearing operations, and payment institutions to conduct cross-border payment business. We will actively promote investment and trade facilitation, and accelerate the reform of integrated regional customs clearance.

Boosting the role of cooperation platforms. A number of international summits, forums, seminars and expos on the theme of the Belt and Road

Initiative have been held, which have played an important role in increasing mutual understanding, reaching consensus and deepening cooperation.

VIII. Embracing a Brighter

Future Together

Though proposed by China, the Belt and Road Initiative is a common aspiration of all countries along their routes. China is ready to conduct equal-footed consultation with all countries along the Belt and Road to seize the opportunity provided by the Initiative, promote opening-up, communication and integration among countries in a larger scope, with higher standards and at deeper levels, while giving consideration to the interests and aspirations of all parties. The development of the Belt and Road is open and inclusive, and we welcome the active participation of all countries and international and regional organizations in this Initiative.

The development of the Belt and Road should mainly be conducted through policy communication and objectives coordination. It is a pluralistic and open process of cooperation which can be highly flexible, and does not seek conformity. China will join other countries along the Belt and Road to substantiate and improve the content and mode of the Belt and Road cooperation, work out relevant timetables and roadmaps, and align national development programs and regional cooperation plans.

China will work with countries along the Belt and Road to carry out joint research, forums and fairs, personnel training, exchanges and visits under the framework of existing bilateral, multilateral, regional and sub-regional cooperation mechanisms, so that they will gain a better understanding and recognition of the contents, objectives and tasks of the Belt and Road Initiative.

China will work with countries along the Belt and Road to steadily advance demonstration projects, jointly identify programs that accommodate bilateral and multilateral interests, and accelerate the launching of programs that are agreed upon by parties and ready for implementation, so as to ensure early harvest.

The Belt and Road cooperation features mutual respect and trust, mutual benefit and win-win cooperation, and mutual learning between civilizations. As long as all countries along the Belt and Road make concerted efforts to pursue our common goal, there will be bright prospects for the Silk Road Economic Belt and the 21st-Century Maritime Silk Road, and the people of countries along the Belt and Road can all benefit from this Initiative.

Press Information Bureau
Government of India
Cabinet

25-March-2015

Sagarmala: Concept and implementation towards Blue Revolution

The Union Cabinet chaired by the Prime Minister, Shri Narendra Modi, today gave its 'in-principle' approval for the concept and institutional framework of Sagarmala Project.

The prime objective of the Sagarmala project is to promote port-led direct and indirect development and to provide infrastructure to transport goods to and from ports quickly, efficiently and cost-effectively. Therefore, the Sagarmala Project shall, inter alia, aim to develop access to new development regions with intermodal solutions and promotion of the optimum modal split, enhanced connectivity with main economic centres and beyond through expansion of rail, inland water, coastal and road services.

The Sagarmala initiative will address challenges by focusing on three pillars of development, namely (i) Supporting and enabling Port-led Development through appropriate policy and institutional interventions and providing for an institutional framework for ensuring inter-agency and ministries/departments/states' collaboration for integrated development, (ii) Port Infrastructure Enhancement, including modernization and setting up of new ports, and (iii) Efficient Evacuation to and from hinterland.

The Sagarmala Project therefore intends to achieve the broad objectives of enhancing the capacity of major and non-major ports and modernizing them to make them efficient, thereby enabling them to become drivers of port-led economic development, optimizing the use of existing and future transport assets and developing new lines/linkages for transport (including roads, rail, inland waterways and coastal routes), setting up of logistics hubs, and establishment of industries and manufacturing centres to be served by ports in EXIM and domestic trade. In addition to strengthening port and evacuation infrastructure, it also aims at simplifying procedures used at ports for cargo movement and promotes usage of electronic channels for information exchange leading to quick, efficient, hassle-free and seamless cargo movement.

For a comprehensive and integrated planning for "Sagarmala", a National Perspective Plan (NPP) for the entire coastline shall be prepared within six months which will identify potential geographical regions to be called Coastal Economic Zones (CEZs). While preparing the NPP, synergy and integration with planned Industrial Corridors, Dedicated Freight Corridors, National Highway Development Programme, Industrial Clusters and SEZs would be ensured. Detailed Master Plans will be prepared for identified Coastal Economic Zones leading to identification of projects and preparation of their detailed project reports.

In order to have effective mechanism at the state level for coordinating and facilitating Sagarmala related projects, the State Governments will be suggested to set up State Sagarmala Committee to be headed by Chief Minister/Minister in Charge of Ports with members from relevant Departments and agencies. The state level Committee will also take up matters on priority as decided in the NSAC. At the state level, the State Maritime Boards/State Port Departments shall service the State Sagarmala Committee and also be, inter alia, responsible for coordination and implementation of individual projects, including through SPVs (as may be necessary) and oversight. The development of each Coastal economic zone shall be done through individual projects and supporting activities that will be undertaken by the State Government, Central line Ministries and SPVs to be formed by the State Governments at the state level or by SDC and ports, as may be necessary.

Sagarmala Coordination and Steering Committee (SCSC) shall be constituted under the chairmanship of the Cabinet Secretary with Secretaries of the Ministries of Shipping, Road Transport and Highways, Tourism, Defence, Home Affairs, Environment, Forest & Climate Change,

Departments of Revenue, Expenditure, Industrial Policy and Promotion, Chairman, Railway Board and CEO, NITI Aayog as members. This Committee will provide coordination between various ministries, state governments and agencies connected with implementation and review the progress of implementation of the National Perspective Plan, Detailed Master Plans and projects. It will, inter alia, consider issues relating to funding of projects and their implementation. This Committee will also examine financing options available for the funding of projects, the possibility of public-private partnership in project financing/construction/ operation.

Improvement of operational efficiency of existing ports, which is an objective of the Sagarmala initiative, shall be done by undertaking business process re-engineering to simplify processes and procedures in addition to modernizing and upgrading the existing infrastructure and improved mechanisation. Increased use of information technology and automation to ensure paperless and seamless transactions will be an important area for intervention. Under the Sagarmala Project, the use of coastal shipping and IWT are proposed to be enhanced through a mix of infrastructure enhancement and policy initiatives.

The Sagarmala initiative would also strive to ensure sustainable development of the population living in the Coastal Economic Zone (CEZ). This would be done by synergising and coordinating with State Governments and line Ministries of Central Government through their existing schemes and programmes such as those related to community and rural development, tribal development and employment generation, fisheries, skill development, tourism promotion etc. In order to provide funding for such projects and activities that may be covered by departmental schemes a separate fund by the name 'Community Development Fund' would be created.

The Institutional Framework for implementing Sagarmala has to provide for a coordinating role for the Central Government. It should provide a platform for central, state governments and local authorities to work in tandem and coordination under the established principles of "cooperative federalism", in order to achieve the objectives of the Sagarmala Project and ensure port-led development.

A National Sagarmala Apex Committee (NSAC) is envisaged for overall policy guidance and high level coordination, and to review various aspects of planning and implementation of the plan and projects. The NSAC shall be chaired by the Minister incharge of Shipping, with Cabinet Ministers from stakeholder Ministries and Chief Ministers/Ministers incharge of ports of maritime states as members. This committee, while providing policy direction and guidance for the initiative's implementation, shall approve the overall National Perspective Plan (NPP) and review the progress of implementation of these plans.

At the Central level, Sagarmala Development Company (SDC) will be set up under the Companies Act, 1956 to assist the State level/zone level Special Purpose Vehicles (SPVs), as well as SPVs to be set up by the ports, with equity support for implementation of projects to be undertaken by them. The SDC shall also get the Detailed Master Plans for individual zones prepared within a two year period. The business plan of the SDC shall be finalised within a period of six months. The SDC will provide a funding window and/or implement only those residual projects that cannot be funded by any other means/mode.

In order to kick start the implementation of projects it is proposed to take up identified projects covered in the concept of Sagarmala for implementation forthwith. These identified projects for implementation in the initial phase will be based on the available data and feasibility study reports and the preparedness, willingness and interest shown by the State Governments and Central Ministries to take up projects.

All efforts would be made to implement those projects through the private sector and through Public Private Participation (PPP) wherever feasible. Funds requirement for starting the implementation of projects in the initial phase of Sagarmala Project is projected at Rs. 692 crores for the FY 2015-16. Further requirement of funds will be finalized after completion of Detailed Master Plan for Coastal Economic Zones for future years. These funds will be used for implementation of projects by line ministries in accordance with approvals by the SCSC.

Background:

Presently, Indian ports handle more than 90 percent of India's total EXIM trade volume. However, the current proportion of merchandize trade in Gross Domestic Product (GDP) of India is only 42 percent, whereas for some developed countries and regions in the world such as Germany and European Union, it is 75 percent and 70 percent respectively. Therefore, there is a great scope to increase the share of merchandising trade in India's GDP. With the Union Government's "Make in India" initiative, the share of merchandise trade in India's GDP is expected to increase and approach levels achieved in developed countries. India lags far behind in ports and logistics infrastructure. Against a share of 9 percent of railways and 6 percent of roads in the GDP the share of ports is only 1 percent. In addition high logistics costs make Indian exports uncompetitive. Therefore Sagarmala project has been envisioned to provide ports and the shipping the rightful place in the Indian economy and to enable port-led development.

Amongst Indian States, Gujarat has been a pioneer in adopting the strategy of port-led development, with significant results. While in the 1980's the state grew at only 5.08 percent per year (National average was 5.47 percent), this accelerated to 8.15 percent per annum in the 1990's (All India average 6.98 percent) and subsequently to more than 10 percent per annum, substantially benefitting from the port-led development model.

The growth of India's maritime sector is constrained due to many developmental, procedural and policy related challenges namely, involvement of multiple agencies in development of infrastructure to promote industrialization, trade, tourism and transportation; presence of a dual institutional structure that has led to development of major and non-major ports as separate, unconnected entities; lack of requisite infrastructure for evacuation from major and non-major ports leading to sub-optimal transport modal mix; limited hinterland linkages that increases the cost of transportation and cargo movement; limited development of centres for manufacturing and urban and economic activities in the hinterland; low penetration of coastal and inland shipping in India, limited mechanization and procedural bottlenecks and lack of scale, deep draft and other facilities at various ports in India.

An illustrative list of the kind of development projects that could be undertaken in Sagarmala initiative are (i) Port-led industrialization (ii) Port based urbanization (iii) Port based and coastal tourism and recreational activities (iv) Short-sea shipping coastal shipping and Inland Waterways Transportation (v) Ship building, ship repair and ship recycling (vi) Logistics parks, warehousing, maritime zones/services (vii) Integration with hinterland hubs (viii) Offshore storage, drilling platforms (ix) Specialization of ports in certain economic activities such as energy, containers, chemicals, coal, agro products, etc. (x) Offshore Renewable Energy Projects with base ports for installations (xi) Modernizing the existing ports and development of new ports. This strategy incorporates both aspects of port-led development viz. port-led direct development and port-led indirect development.

PROGRESS OF TRILATERAL ROAD

July 31, 2014
RAJYA SABHA

PROGRESS OF TRILATERAL ROAD

(a) the Status of progress of Trilateral road proposed to be built in India, Myanmar and Thailand;

(b) the length of the total roads with the country-wise break up in terms of length, cost and progress so far; and

(c) the deadline set for completion of the project and measures, if any, to speed up the project?

(Source:http://www.mea.gov.in/rajyasabha.htm?dtl/23789/Q+2343+PRO GRESS+OF+TRILATERAL+ROAD)

THE MINISTER OF STATE IN THE MINISTRY OF EXTERNAL AFFAIRS

[GEN. (DR) V. K. SINGH (RETD)]

(a) & (b) The length of the Trilateral Highway is approximately 1360 kms. The Trilateral Highway's route will be Moreh (India) – Tamu (Myanmar) – Kalewa – Yagyi – Monywa – Mandalay – Meiktila – Nay Pyi Taw – Payagyi – Theinzayat – Thaton – Hpa'an – Kawkareik – Myawaddy (Myanmar) – Mae Sot (Thailand). In respect of India's involvement with the project, India has undertaken to upgrade the Kalewa-Yagyi road section of the Trilateral Highway (approximately 120 kms) to highway standard and construction of 71 bridges in the Tamu – Kalewa section. A consultant, M/s EGIS India Consulting Engineers Private Ltd., has been appointed on January 28, 2014 for preparation of a Feasibility Report for the Kalewa – Yagyi road section. A consultant, M/s IRCON Ltd., has been appointed on February 12, 2014 for preparation of a Feasibility Report for the construction of 71 bridges in the Tamu-Kalewa section of the Trilateral Highway. These two Feasibility Reports will provide the broad contours of the project including alignment, specifications, design, estimated cost and timeline for completion of these projects.

(c) The two Feasibility Reports will provide the broad contours of the projects including specifications, design, estimated cost and timeline for completion of these projects. Based on the two Feasibility Reports, implementation of these projects will be finalized in consultation with the Government of Myanmar.

(Source: http://pib.nic.in/newsite/PrintRelease.aspx?relid=117691 &\ http://pibphoto.nic.in/documents/rlink/2016/apr/p201641402.pdf)

Index

www.ingramcontent.com/pod-product-compliance
Lightning Source LLC
Chambersburg PA
CBHW021537260326
41914CB00001B/51